CAJUN COOKING

CAJUN COOKING

From Gumbo to Jambalaya, bring the traditional tastes of Louisiana to your kitchen with 50 authentic Cajun and Creole recipes, shown in 250 photographs

Ruby Le Bois

southwater

This edition is published by Southwater, an imprint of Anness Publishing Ltd,
Blaby Road, Wigston, Leicestershire LE18 4SE; info@anness.com

www.southwaterbooks.com; www.annesspublishing.com

If you like the images in this book and would like to investigate using them for publishing,
promotions or advertising, please visit our website www.practicalpictures.com for more information.

Publisher: Joanna Lorenz
Project Editors: Clare Nicholson and Kate Eddison
Designer: David Rowley
Jacket Design: Peter Butler
Photographer: James Duncan
Home Economist: Jane Hartshorn
Production Manager: Steve Lang

ACKNOWLEDGEMENTS

The publishers would like to thank the following for permission to reproduce their images:
6 (top) iStockphoto, 6 (bottom) Antonio Abrignani/Shutterstock, 7 Inggita Notosusanto/Shutterstock,
8 (bottom) pisaphotography/Shutterstock, as well as Prestige Housewares for the loan of products
for the step-by-step photography.

PUBLISHER'S NOTE
Although the advice and information in this book are believed to be accurate and true at the
time of going to press, neither the authors nor the publisher can accept any legal responsibility or liability
for any errors or omissions that may have been made nor for any inaccuracies nor for any loss, harm or
injury that comes about from following instructions or advice in this book.

NOTES
Bracketed terms are intended for American readers.
For all recipes, quantities are given in both metric and imperial measures and, where appropriate, in standard
cups and spoons. Follow one set of measures, but not a mixture, because they are not interchangeable.
Standard spoon and cup measures are level. 1 tsp = 5ml, 1 tbsp = 15ml, 1 cup = 250ml/8fl oz.
Australian standard tablespoons are 20ml. Australian readers should use 3 tsp in place of 1 tbsp for measuring small quantities.
American pints are 16fl oz/2 cups. American readers should use 20fl oz/2.5 cups in place of 1 pint when measuring liquids.
Electric oven temperatures in this book are for conventional ovens.
When using a fan oven, the temperature will probably need to be reduced by about 10–20°C/20–40°F.
Since ovens vary, you should check with your manufacturer's instruction book for guidance.
The nutritional analysis given for each recipe is calculated per portion (i.e. serving or item), unless otherwise stated.
If the recipe gives a range, such as Serves 4–6, then the nutritional analysis will be for the smaller portion size, i.e. 6 servings.
The analysis does not include optional ingredients, such as salt added to taste.
Medium (US large) eggs are used unless otherwise stated.
Main front cover image shows Louisiana Seafood Gumbo – for recipe, see page 34.

Contents

Introduction

EUROPEANS of aristocratic descent established plantations in Louisiana around the beginning of the seventeenth century, and set about enjoying an elegant life-style with plenty of servants to run their households as well as pick their cotton. For two hundred years the French and Spanish governed Louisiana by turns, and their cooks learned to switch from one cuisine to another, substituting native staples like corn and cayenne for less available wheat and black pepper, and occasionally introducing their own native African ingredients, such as okra, into the cooking pot. It is this mixing of European with indigenous and African culinary traditions that produces the style known as Creole.

American Creole cooking was born and grew up in New Orleans. It was city food, sophisticated and refined to please the palates of the wealthy families for whom it was created. New Orleans prospered and became a hub of wealth-generating commerce: by 1850, half the millionaires in the United States had property around the city.

Those fine gentlemen who set up elegant homes along the Mississippi wanted grand restaurants in which

to entertain, and by the turn of the century establishments such as Antoine's were already thriving. Antoine's still flourishes today, joined by a host of others, from the Commander's Palace in the smart Garden District of the city and Lafitte's Landing at Donaldsonville, to Paul Prudhomme's K-Paul's Louisiana Kitchen in the jazzy heart of New Orleans, where the decor is homelier but the food is so good that a queue for lunch starts forming around 11am (K-Paul's takes no bookings).

Above: Jackson Square in the historic French Quarter of New Orleans.

Cajun cooking, although also French-based, is a hearty, agrarian culinary style of quite different pedigree. The word Cajun is a corruption of the prettier "Acadian", and the first Acadia was in Nova Scotia, peopled from 1620 by French peasant farmers and fishermen. They brought their own culinary traditions with them from France, but adapted them to a new and unfamiliar set of ingredients. Then, in the mid-eighteenth century, these Roman Catholic Acadians found themselves once more displaced, this time exiled by British colonialists.

Communities and families were split up as men were first shipped out in one direction, then women and children herded off in another. Eventually a number found their way to "the French triangle" of South-West Louisiana, once more hooked their big black iron cooking pots over their fires, and looked around their new Acadia for something to put in them. There was plenty for those who knew where to look, and these first Cajuns, whose forefathers had already proved their survival skills in an unfamiliar

Left: Depiction of the New Orleans port from a mid-19th century photograph.

Right: Colourful spices and vegetables adorn the outside of a local store.

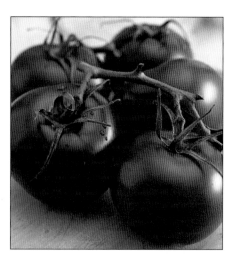

Above, left to right: Green, yellow and red (bell) peppers, corn and tomatoes.

environment, again set about adapting their culinary technique to a new set of ingredients.

For those near the coast there was seafood aplenty, while further inland the bayous were teeming with sweet-water fish, including the crawfish that is still a signature of Cajun cooking. There was big game – bear as well as deer – and plenty of wild fowl. There were wild vegetables, herbs and fruits to be gathered, and native Americans to teach them where to find them and how best to use them, sensing no threat from such hard-working peasant settlers. By the middle of this century these two cuisines, the Cajun and the Creole, both born on American soil of European ancestry, had begun to merge, at least in the minds of the increasing stream of visiting pilgrims to the birthplace of jazz. Maybe you could tell Cajun cooking from Creole at the home hearth, but in the restaurants where visitors ate, distinctions became blurred.

Below: A street car in the famous streets of New Orleans.

In the decades that followed the jetpowered explosion of tourism, full-blooded Cajun cooks like Paul Prudhomme joined the restaurant boom, and found it necessary to adapt the long, slow cooking style of their forebears to fit the demands to a fast-paced restaurant kitchen. Faster heat meant shorter cooking times, a principle that reached its apotheosis in the blackening technique; blackened redfish, considered by many visitors the foundation stone of Cajun cooking, was a dish invented by Paul Prudhomme in 1979. In 1983, Paul Prudhomme cooked for visiting heads of state at Ronald Reagan's 1983 Williamsburg summit, and Cajun cuisine was catapulted into the worldwide limelight.

While international marketing was playing its part in corrupting Cajun cooking to fit the new hot culinary fashion, Prudhomme and his contemporaries were at their stoves evolving a new, authentic Louisiana cooking that married the old styles of Cajun and Creole, while taking advantage of ingredients made available by jet-set freighting and the new interstate highways already criss-crossing the bayous. This New Louisiana cooking is a true descendant of the American–European heritage, its hallmark exciting but judicious pepper-spicing, using Old World black and white peppercorns as well as the huge native American range of red capsicum, and emphasizing always the freshness of available ingredients.

Above, left to right: Okra, chillies and cayenne pepper.

One of the exponents of the New Louisiana style, John Folse, chef at Lafitte's Landing restaurant, explained on a visit to London, where he cooked for food- and travel writers, that the heredity of the cuisine was entirely based on adaptation. What is one person's trash food is another's luxury. The first Cajun settlers found the shoreline awash with oysters and lobsters, so that is what they used. If they had found mussels they would undoubtedly have used those. It is a happy-go-lucky, permissive message to give to cooks who want the adventure of Louisiana food: go ahead, and use what is around you. Just make sure it is good and fresh, and cook it with love.

Roux

Roux is a crucial ingredient in many Cajun and Creole dishes. It is a thickener and a flavouring agent, and it needs to be cooked slowly and with constant attention. Heat the oil in a large, heavy pan, and, when it is hot, add the flour and stir constantly with a wooden spoon or whisk until it reaches the desired colour. It is vital to stir constantly to darken the roux without burning. Should black specks occur at any stage of cooking, you must discard the roux and start it again.

Top Left: Light Brown
Top Right: Peanut Butter Brown
Bottom Left: Dark Nutty Brown
Bottom Right: Black

Appetizers, Snacks & Sauces

All the ingredients you need for tasty appetizers, snacks and sauces are abundant in Louisiana – seafood in vast quantity and variety, sweet peppers, splendid salad greens, luscious tomatoes and golden corn.

Many of the vegetable dishes of the area are shown off best in the stand-alone status of appetizer or light meal, perhaps with a salad garnish, as in the case of Hot Parsnip Fritters and Creole Cheese Potato Puffs, or in combination with each other, like Corn Cakes with Grilled Tomatoes.

These are the sort of dishes to evoke the Louisiana ambiance of a meal, and indeed they are even setting the standards for a new style of dining in Cajun country.

Beignets

In New Orleans, where a night on the town really can last all night, revellers are glad of a pit-stop at the Café du Monde, which serves its popular treats of 'café au lait' and sugary beignets 24 hours a day. Chef John False of Lafitte's Landing restaurant, who is deeply interested in Louisiana history, says the recipe for these doughy delights was brought to Louisiana in 1727 by Ursuline nuns. This is his version of their recipe.

MAKES 20

INGREDIENTS
1 packet active dried yeast
400g/14oz/3½ cups plain
*   (all-purpose) flour*
5ml/1 tsp salt
50g/2oz/1¼ cup caster (superfine) sugar
300ml/10fl oz/1¼ cups milk
3 eggs, beaten
25g/1oz/2 tbsp butter, melted
oil, for deep-frying
115g/4oz/1 cup icing
*   (confectioners') sugar*

1 Dissolve the yeast in 60ml/4 tbsp warm water and set aside.

2 In a large mixing bowl, combine the flour, salt and caster sugar and mix well. Fold in the dissolved yeast, milk, eggs and melted butter.

3 Continue to mix until a smooth dough is formed.

4 Knead the dough until smooth and elastic. Cover the dough with a towel and leave to rise in a warm place for 1 hour.

5 Roll out the dough to 5mm/¼in thick on a well-floured surface. Cut into rectangular shapes about 5 × 7.5cm/ 2 × 3in and put them in a lightly floured Swiss roll tin (jelly roll pan).

6 Cover with a towel and leave to rise in a warm place for an hour or until they have both doubled in bulk.

7 Put the icing sugar into a deep dish or oven tin. Heat the oil for deep-frying and fry the beignets in batches, turning each, until golden brown on both sides. Drain well on kitchen paper.

8 As each batch of beignets is cooked, transfer with a slotted spoon to the icing sugar, and shake them about to coat the beignets liberally.

COOK'S TIP

The important thing with beignets, as with all doughnuts, is to have the oil at the right temperature to cook the dough right through to the middle before the outside is too dark brown.

Treat the first beignet or two as a test. Break them open, and if they are still sticky in the middle, lower the heat and allow the oil to cool down a little before continuing with the next batch.

Eat the beignets soon after cooking, and certainly on the same day as they are made.

Creole Omelette

SERVES 3–4

INGREDIENTS
*1 large Spanish (Bermuda) onion,
    finely chopped
25g/1oz/2 tbsp butter
1 garlic clove, crushed
15ml/2 tbsp soft white breadcrumbs
4 large tomatoes, skinned and chopped
50g/2oz/½ cup lean cooked ham,
    finely chopped
salt, freshly ground black and
    cayenne peppers
6 eggs, lightly beaten
chopped fresh parsley, to garnish*

1 Soften the onion in the butter in a heavy frying pan, stirring regularly over a low heat for about 10 minutes.

2 Add the garlic and breadcrumbs, and continue to stir over the heat until the breadcrumbs begin to crisp.

3 Add the tomatoes and cook for 10–15 minutes until they have broken down. Stir in the ham and season the mixture quite highly to compensate for the eggs.

4 Preheat the grill. Stir the beaten eggs through the mixture and continue to stir over the heat, breaking up the base as it sets to allow the uncooked mixture to move through.

5 When the omelette begins to set, leave to cook over a low heat until almost completely set.

6 Put the omelette under a preheated grill (broiler) to cook the top. Serve either whole on a warm serving plate or direct from the pan, cut in wedges. Garnish with chopped parsley.

COOK'S TIP

For a spicier dish, you can replace the ham with cut-up spicy sausages. You can also omit the ham altogether, to make the omelette suitable for vegetarians.

Muffuletto Sandwich

In New Orleans you buy your Muffuletto sandwich ready-made from one of the grocery stores on Chartres Street that are famous for it, and where they also make up the olive pickle (an essential ingredient) by the barrel-load. There it comes in a special 25cm/10in diameter soft loaf, like an extra large hamburger bun, served in quarters. You can make it at home in a baguette or French loaf.

SERVES 4

INGREDIENTS
For the olive pickle
1 celery stick, finely chopped
1 garlic clove, crushed
1 canned red (bell) pepper, drained and finely chopped
75g/3oz/⅔ cup pitted green olives, chopped
15ml/ 2 tbsp pickled cocktail onions, drained and coarsely chopped
10ml/2 tsp capers, drained and halved
45ml/3 tbsp olive oil
10ml/2 tsp red wine vinegar

For the sandwich
1 large baguette
4 thin slices prosciutto
50g/2oz Provolone or Emmental cheese, thinly sliced
50g/2oz Italian salami, rinded and thinly sliced black pepper, for grinding

1 Mix all the vegetable and pickled ingredients for the olive pickle, then stir in the oil and vinegar and refrigerate well.

2 To make the sandwich, halve the baguette and cut it lengthways. Line the base with prosciutto. Lay the cheese on top and grind on some black pepper, then overlay with slices of salami.

3 Finally spoon the olive pickle on top of the salami and press the sandwich shut.

Eggs Sardou

Restaurants do not come and go much in New Orleans: Antoine's, where this dish was created in 1908, is still there, right in the heart of jazzland. This dish's popularity has spread and it now crops up on brunch menus as well as being a favourite appetizer.

SERVES 4

INGREDIENTS

4 large fresh artichokes
500g/1¼lb fresh spinach
50g/2oz/4 tbsp butter
30ml/2 tbsp plain (all-purpose) flour
175ml/6fl oz/¾ cup milk
4 canned anchovy fillets, drained and mashed
salt, freshly ground black pepper, grated nutmeg and Tabasco sauce
4 eggs

For the Hollandaise sauce
30ml/2 tbsp white wine vinegar
4 black peppercorns
1 bay leaf
2 egg yolks, at room temperature
115g/4oz/½ cup butter, at warm room temperature, cubed
salt and freshly ground black pepper

1 With a sharp knife, cut the stems from the artichokes, then cut off the top half of each artichoke and scoop out the fibrous centre. Set aside.

2 Wash the spinach thoroughly, trimming off any discoloured areas, as well as the coarser stems. Put the spinach into a deep pan with just the water that clings to it. Cover and cook until it wilts completely. Turn out into a colander and, when cool enough to handle, squeeze out much of the moisture. Slice across the ball of spinach both ways to chop it.

3 To make the Hollandaise sauce, boil the vinegar with 2 tsp water, the peppercorns and bay leaf in a small pan until the liquid is reduced to 1 tbsp. Leave to cool.

4 Cream the egg yolks with one cube of soft butter and a pinch of salt in a heatproof bowl, then strain the vinegar over, set the bowl over a pan of boiling water and turn off the heat.

5 Whisk in the remaining butter a cube at a time, adding each cube as the one before melts into the sauce. Carry on whisking until the sauce is shiny and thick. Season with salt and pepper. Leave over the pan of water to keep warm.

6 Bring a large pan full of salted water to the boil. Add the artichokes, cover and cook for about 30 minutes or until tender. Lift them with a slotted spoon on to warmed serving plates and keep warm.

7 Meanwhile, to finish the spinach, melt the butter in a wide pan, mix in the flour and stir for 1 minute over the heat until the roux froths and bubbles. Take off the heat and pour in the milk gradually, stirring constantly. When the sauce loosens, return it to the heat and continue stirring in the milk.

8 When the sauce reaches simmering point, stir in the mashed anchovies and leave to simmer for about 5 minutes. Then add the chopped spinach, return to simmering point, season with black pepper, nutmeg, Tabasco sauce and salt if it needs it, and keep warm.

9 Poach the eggs 2 at a time in the pan of artichoke cooking water.

10 To assemble the dish, spoon some spinach into each artichoke, allowing it to spill over the edges. Set a poached egg on the plate and spoon Hollandaise sauce over.

Cream of Red Pepper Soup

Grilling peppers gives them a smoky sweetness that is delicious in salads or, as here, in a velvety soup with a secret flavouring of rosemary to add resinous depth. This soup is equally good served hot or chilled.

SERVES 4

INGREDIENTS

4 red (bell) peppers
1 onion, finely chopped
25g/1oz/2 tbsp butter
1 sprig fresh rosemary
1.2 litres/2 pints/5 cups chicken or light
  vegetable stock
45ml/3 tbsp tomato purée (paste)
120ml/4fl oz/½ cup double
  (heavy) cream
salt, freshly ground black pepper
  and paprika

COOK'S TIP

Use vegetable rather than chicken stock to make the soup suitable for vegetarians.

1 Preheat the grill (broiler). Put the peppers in the grill (broiling) pan under the hot grill and turn them regularly until the skins have blackened all round. Put them into polythene bags, sealing them closed. Leave them for 20 minutes.

2 Flake the blackened skin off the peppers, avoiding rinsing them under the tap if possible as this loses some of the natural oil and hence the flavour.

3 Halve the peppers, removing the seeds, stalks and pith, then roughly chop the flesh.

4 Melt the butter in a deep pan. Add the onion and rosemary, and cook gently over a low heat for about 5 minutes. Remove the rosemary from the pan and discard.

5 Add the peppers and stock to the onion, bring to the boil and simmer for 15 minutes. Stir in the tomato purée, then process the soup until smooth, or strain through a sieve (strainer).

6 Stir in half the cream and season with salt, if necessary, with pepper and a little paprika.

7 Serve the soup hot or chilled, with the remaining cream swirled delicately on top. Speckle the cream very lightly with a sprinkling of paprika.

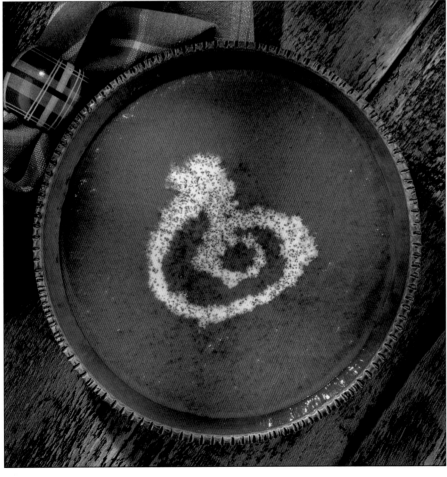

Creole Onion Soup

SERVES 4

INGREDIENTS
50g/2oz/4 tbsp butter
2 large onions, quartered and thinly sliced
1 bay leaf
45ml/3 tbsp plain (all-purpose) flour
1 litre/1¾ pints/4½ cups chicken stock
75g/3oz/¾ cup grated Cheddar cheese
30ml/2 tbsp bourbon
120ml/4 fl oz/½ cup milk
salt and freshly ground black pepper

3 Gradually add the remaining stock, then bring to the boil, partially cover and simmer for 20 minutes.

4 Add the bourbon to the pan, return to the boil, and cook for 1 minute. Stir in the milk. Return once more to simmering point, remove the bay leaf, and correct the seasoning to taste with salt, if necessary, and plenty of black pepper.

5 Ladle the soup into bowls and sprinkle each portion with a little of the remaining grated Cheddar.

1 Melt the butter in a deep pan, add the onions and bay leaf, and cook over a very low heat for about 20 minutes, until the onions are very soft and mushy, but not darkened beyond pale gold in colour.

2 Sprinkle on the flour and return to the heat, stirring until the flour is well amalgamated, then lift the pan off the heat and stir in 250ml/8fl oz/ 1 cup of the stock, a little at a time. Return to the heat and stir until it thickens smoothly. Add 50g/2oz/½ cup of the cheese and continue stirring gently until it melts.

Hot Parsnip Fritters on Baby Spinach

Fritters are naturally a favourite of Cajun cooks, with their love for deep-frying. The technique brings out the luscious sweetness of parsnips, here set, none too traditionally, on a walnut-dressed salad of baby spinach leaves.

SERVES 4

INGREDIENTS
2 large parsnips
1 egg, separated
115g/4oz/1 cup plain (all-purpose) flour
120ml/4fl oz/½ cup milk
salt, freshly ground black pepper
*   and cayenne pepper*
115g/4oz baby spinach leaves
30ml/2 tbsp olive oil
15ml/1 tbsp walnut oil
15ml/1 tbsp sherry vinegar
oil, for deep-frying
15ml/1 tbsp coarsely chopped walnuts

1 Peel the parsnips, bring to the boil in a pan of salted water and simmer for 10–15 minutes until tender but not in the least mushy. Drain, cool and cut diagonally into slices about 5cm/2in long × 5mm–1cm/¼–½in thick.

2 Put the egg yolk into a well in the flour in a bowl and mix in with a fork, gradually pulling in the surrounding flour. Begin adding the milk, while continuing to mix in the flour. Season with salt, ground black pepper and cayenne pepper, and beat with a whisk until the batter is smooth.

3 Wash and dry the spinach leaves and put them in a bowl. In a screwtop bottle, mix the olive and walnut oils, sherry vinegar, salt and pepper.

4 When you are ready to serve, whisk the egg white to the soft-peak stage. Fold in a little of the yolk batter, then gently fold all of the white into the batter. Heat the oil for frying.

5 Meanwhile, shake the dressing bottle vigorously, then toss the salad in the dressing. Arrange the dressed leaves on 4 salad plates and sprinkle with walnuts.

6 Dip the parsnip slices in batter and fry a few at a time until puffy and golden. Drain on kitchen paper and keep warm. To serve, arrange the fritters on top of the salad leaves.

Eggs in Remoulade Sauce

There are as many recipes for Remoulade sauce as there are cooks in Louisiana. This one comes from the McIlhenny family, makers of Tabasco sauce. Naturally they splash some of the hot stuff into their Remoulade.

SERVES 4

INGREDIENTS

45ml/3 tbsp coarse-ground mustard
10ml/2 tsp paprika
5ml/1 tsp Tabasco sauce
5ml/1 tsp salt
2.5ml/½ tsp freshly ground black pepper
45ml/3 tbsp tarragon vinegar
250ml/8fl oz/1 cup olive oil
3 spring onions (scallions), shredded
1 celery stick, shredded
45ml/3 tbsp finely chopped fresh parsley
6 hard-boiled eggs
mustard and cress (fine-curled cress), to garnish

1 Whisk together the mustard, paprika, Tabasco sauce, salt and pepper, then beat in the vinegar.

2 Beating constantly, add the oil slowly in a thin trickle, continuing to beat until the sauce is thick and smooth.

COOK'S TIP

This is an easy dish to make in a larger quantity for a buffet table. Leave the final assembly as late as you can before serving.

3 Stir in the spring onions, celery and parsley, and mix well. Cover the bowl and leave to stand for at least 2 hours to allow the flavours to blend.

4 Meanwhile, shell the eggs and halve them lengthways. Arrange 3 halves on each of 4 side plates, or pile them all up to serve at the table. Spoon the sauce over, then sprinkle lightly with mustard and cress.

Corn Cakes with Grilled Tomatoes

SERVES 4

INGREDIENTS

1 large cob fresh corn
75g/3oz/³⁄₄ cup plain (all-purpose) flour
1 egg
a little milk
salt and freshly ground black pepper
2 large firm tomatoes
1 garlic clove
5ml/1 tsp dried oregano
45ml/3 tbsp oil, plus extra for
  shallow-frying
8 cupped leaves iceberg lettuce
shredded fresh basil leaves, to garnish

1 Pull the husks and silk away from the corn, then hold the cob upright on a board and cut downwards with a heavy knife to strip off the kernels. Put the kernels into a pan of boiling water and cook for 3 minutes after the water has returned to the boil, then drain and rinse under the cold tap to cool quickly.

2 Put the flour into a bowl and break the egg into a well in the middle, then stir in the flour slowly with a fork, adding a little milk to make a soft dropping consistency. Stir in the drained corn and season.

3 Preheat the grill (broiler). Halve the tomatoes horizontally and make 2 or 3 criss-cross slashes across the cut side of each half. Crush the garlic and rub it, the oregano and some salt and pepper over the cut surface of each half, then trickle with oil and grill (broil) until lightly browned.

4 While the tomatoes grill, heat some oil in a wide frying pan and drop a tablespoonful of batter into the centre. Cook, one at a time, over a low heat and turn as soon as the top is set. Drain on kitchen paper and keep warm while cooking the remaining fritters. The mixture should make at least 8 corn cakes.

5 Put 2 corn cakes on to lettuce leaves, garnish with basil and serve with a grilled (broiled) tomato half.

Green Herb Gumbo

Traditionally served at the end of Lent, this is a joyful, sweetly spiced and revitalizing dish, even if you have not been fasting. The variety of green ingredients is important, so buy substitutes if you cannot find all of them.

SERVES 6–8

INGREDIENTS
350g/12oz piece raw smoked gammon (smoked cured ham)
30ml/2 tbsp lard, white cooking fat or oil
1 large Spanish (Bermuda) onion, chopped
2–3 garlic cloves, crushed
5ml/1 tsp dried oregano
5ml/1 tsp dried thyme
2 bay leaves
2 cloves
2 celery sticks, finely sliced
1 green (bell) pepper, seeded and chopped
½ medium green cabbage, stalked and finely shredded
2 litres/3½ pints/9 cups light stock or water
200g/7oz spring greens (collards) or kale, finely shredded
200g/7oz Chinese mustard greens, finely shredded (see Cook's Tip)
200g/7oz spinach, shredded
1 bunch watercress, shredded
6 spring onions (scallions), finely shredded
25g/1oz/½ cup chopped fresh parsley
2.5ml/½ tsp ground allspice
1.5ml/¼ nutmeg, grated
salt, freshly ground black pepper and cayenne pepper
hot French bread or garlic bread, to serve

COOK'S TIP

Chinese mustard greens are increasingly available in supermarkets, as well as from oriental shops and markets. If, however, you cannot find them, substitute turnip tops or kohlrabi leaves.

1 Cut the ham into small dice, keeping any fat and rind in one separate piece. Put the fat piece with the lard or oil into a deep pan and heat until it sizzles. Stir in the diced ham, onion, garlic, oregano and thyme and stir over a medium heat for 5 minutes.

2 Add the bay leaves, cloves, celery and green pepper and stir for 2–3 minutes more over the heat, then add the cabbage and stock or water. Bring to the boil and simmer for 5 minutes.

3 Add the spring greens or kale and mustard greens, boil for a further 2 minutes, then add the spinach, watercress and spring onions and lower the heat. Simmer for 1 minute after it returns to the boil, then add the parsley, ground allspice and nutmeg, salt, black pepper and cayenne pepper to taste.

4 Remove the piece of ham fat and, if you can find them, the cloves. Serve immediately, with hot French bread or garlic bread.

Corn and Crab Bisque

A Louisiana classic, and certainly luxurious enough for a dinner party, which makes it worth the trouble. The crab shells together with the corn cobs, from which the kernels are stripped, make a fine-flavoured stock.

SERVES 8

INGREDIENTS
*4 large cobs corn
2 bay leaves
salt, freshly ground black and white
    pepper, and cayenne pepper
1 cooked crab, weighing about 1kg/2¼lb
25g/1oz/2 tbsp butter
30ml/2 tbsp plain (all-purpose) flour
300ml/10fl oz/1¼ cups whipping cream
6 spring onions (scallions), shredded
hot French bread or grissini bread sticks,
    to serve*

1 Pull away the husks and silk from the cobs of corn and strip off the kernels (see step 1 of Corn Cakes with Grilled Tomatoes, for the method).

2 Set the kernels aside and put the stripped cobs into a deep pan or flame-proof casserole with 3 litres/5 pints/12½ cups cold water, the bay leaves and 10ml/2 tsp salt. Bring to the boil, cover and leave to simmer while you prepare the crab.

3 Pull away the two flaps between the big claws of the crab, stand it on its 'nose' where the flaps were and bang down firmly with the heel of your hand on the rounded end.

4 Separate the crab from its top shell, keeping the shell.

5 Push out the crab's mouth and its abdominal sac immediately below the mouth, and discard.

6 Pull away the feathery gills surrounding the central chamber and discard. Scrape out all the semi-liquid brown meat from the shell and reserve.

7 Crack the claws in as many places as necessary to extract all the white meat. Pick out the white meat from the fragile cavities in the central body of the crab. Set aside all the crabmeat, brown and white. Put the spidery legs, back shell and all the other pieces of shell into the pan with the corn cobs. Simmer for a further 15 minutes, then strain the stock into a clean pan and boil hard to reduce to 2 litres/3½ pints/9 cups.

8 Meanwhile, melt the butter in a small pan and sprinkle in the flour. Stir constantly over a low heat to make a roux. Stir until the roux is the colour of rich cream (*see* Introduction).

9 Off the heat, slowly stir in 250ml/8fl oz/1 cup of the stock. Return to the heat and stir until it thickens, then stir this thickened mixture into the pot of strained stock.

10 Add the corn kernels, return to the boil and simmer for 5 minutes.

11 Add the crabmeat, cream and spring onions and season with salt, black or white pepper (or a bit of both) and cayenne pepper. Return to the boil and simmer for a further 2 minutes. Serve with hot French bread or grissini bread sticks.

COOK'S TIP

You can, if you prefer, ask your fishmonger to remove all the inedible bits of the crab – the mouth, stomach sac and gills. You will need the shell and spidery legs for the stock.

Prawn and Artichoke Salad

Artichokes are a very popular Louisiana ingredient – and the local cooks use canned hearts in the best of circles.

SERVES 4

INGREDIENTS
1 garlic clove
salt and freshly ground black pepper
10ml/2 tsp Dijon mustard
60ml/4 tbsp red wine vinegar
150ml/5fl oz/²⁄₃ cup olive oil
45ml/3 tbsp shredded fresh basil leaves
*   or 30ml/2 tbsp finely chopped*
*   fresh parsley*
1 red onion, very finely sliced
350g/12oz cooked shelled prawns (shrimp)
400g/14oz can artichoke hearts
½ head iceberg lettuce

1 Chop the garlic, then crush it to a pulp with 1 tsp salt, using the flat of a heavy knife blade.

2 Mix the garlic and mustard to a paste, then beat in the vinegar and finally the olive oil, beating hard to make a thick creamy dressing. Season with black pepper and, if necessary, additional salt.

3 Stir the basil or parsley into the dressing, followed by the sliced onion. Leave to stand for 30 minutes at room temperature, then stir in the prawns and refrigerate for 1 hour or until ready to serve.

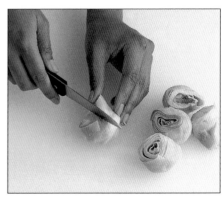

4 Drain the artichoke hearts and halve each one. Shred the lettuce finely.

5 Make a bed of lettuce on a serving platter or 4 individual salad plates, and spread the artichoke hearts over it.

6 Immediately before serving, pour the prawns and onion and their marinade over the top of the salad.

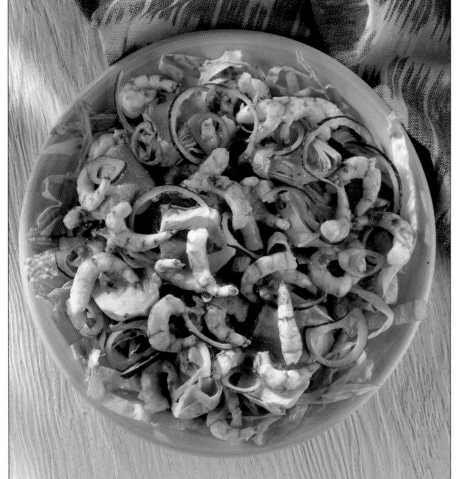

Creole Cheese Potato Puffs

It is worth boiling extra potatoes just to have some left over to mash for this heartening and tasty appetizer.

SERVES 4–6

INGREDIENTS
45ml/3 tbsp milk
25g/1oz/2 tbsp butter
450g/1lb/2½ cups cold mashed potatoes
50g/2oz/½ cup grated Cheddar cheese
4 spring onions (scallions), shredded
salt, freshly ground black pepper and grated nutmeg
2 eggs, separated
watercress and cherry tomatoes, to garnish

1 Preheat the oven to 220°C/425°F/ Gas 7 and generously butter a 12-hole non-stick muffin pan, buttering the sections between the indents as well.

2 Warm the milk and butter to just below boiling point in a small pan, then mix thoroughly into the mashed potatoes with the cheese, spring onions and seasoning. Mix in the egg yolks and beat thoroughly.

COOK'S TIP

Garnished elegantly, these puffs make a pretty appetizer, but on a more homely occasion they are just as good served with sausages and tomato ketchup.

3 Whisk the egg whites to the soft-peak stage. Mix a tablespoonful or two of the whites thoroughly into the potato mixture to loosen it, then fold the rest of the whites through the potato as lightly as you can.

4 Spoon the mixture into the muffin pan and bake in the oven for about 15 minutes, until the puffs have risen and are tinged golden brown. Serve immediately, garnished with fresh watercress and cherry tomatoes.

Red Pepper Jelly

A sweet-savoury jelly that is good with pork, lamb and duck. Serve it at the table to spoon out alongside the meat, or use it as a glaze for grilled cuts (see the recipe for Duck Breasts with Red Pepper Jelly glaze). It is also good with a sharp cheese such as mature Cheddar.

MAKES ABOUT 1.5kg/3lb

INGREDIENTS
1kg/2¼lb eating apples
juice of 1 lemon
1kg/2¼lb/5 cups granulated (white) sugar
115g/4oz red chilli peppers, seeded and roughly chopped
1 large red (bell) pepper, seeded and roughly chopped
1 large Spanish (Bermuda) onion, chopped
350ml/12fl oz/1½ cups cider vinegar

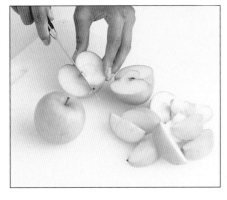

1 Cut each apple into about 8 pieces, discarding only the bruised and damaged sections, not the cores, peel, seeds or stems. Put into a large, deep pan with the lemon juice and 1 litre/1¾ pints/4½ cups cold water. Bring to the boil, cover and simmer for 30 minutes.

2 Line a colander with a clean dish towel and set it over a deep bowl. Pour the apples and liquid into this and leave to drip through undisturbed.

3 Discard the apple debris and pour the liquid into a pan with 800g/1¾lb/ 4 cups of the sugar. Stir over a low heat until the sugar dissolves completely and the liquid clears. Raise the heat and boil without further stirring until a little of the syrup, spread on a cold plate, wrinkles when you push it with your finger. Start testing after 15 minutes, but anticipate that it may take 30 minutes.

4 Either mince (grind) or process the red chilli peppers, red peppers and onion together to create a fine hash.

5 Stir the vegetables, vinegar and the remaining sugar together in a large pan over a low heat until the sugar dissolves. Raise the heat as boiling point approaches and boil for 5 minutes, then add to the apple syrup and once again boil until the mixture passes the wrinkle test.

6 Ladle the jelly into hot sterilized jars, cover with vinegar-proof discs and lids and cool for about 20 minutes, then invert the jars to redistribute the flecks of pepper. After a further 20 minutes turn them the right way up to complete the cooling process. Wipe away any external stickiness with a hot damp cloth, then label. Store in a cool place. The jelly should keep for up to 1 year.

Cajun Bloody Mary

It was in New York that the life-enhancing dash of Tabasco was first added to the classic morning-after reviver. In Cajun country they make their Bloody Marys by the pitcherful.

SERVES 6

INGREDIENTS
250ml/8fl oz/1 cup vodka
30ml/2 tbsp fresh lime juice
15ml/1 tbsp Worcestershire sauce
1 litre/1¾ pints/4½ cups tomato
   juice, chilled
celery salt and black pepper
4–6 dashes Tabasco sauce
ice cubes and celery sticks, to serve

I Mix the vodka, lime juice and Worcestershire sauce thoroughly in a measuring cup, then stir into the chilled tomato juice in a pitcher.

2 Season to taste with celery salt, black pepper and Tabasco sauce and stir very thoroughly with a long spoon.

3 Pour over ice cubes in chunky tumblers and serve with a celery stick, preferably with a bit of greenery attached, as a stirrer, in each glass.

Avery Island Salsa

Tabasco sauce is made, as it has been for over a century, by the McIlhenny family on Avery Island off the coast of Louisiana. The present generation of McIlhennys has concocted a thick and spicy salsa, which keeps up to five days in the refrigerator. But be warned – they like it hot on Avery Island. Cut down on the Tabasco for a milder salsa. This is great with all grilled food, and even better with barbecued meat.

MAKES 600ml/1 pint/2½ cups

INGREDIENTS
30ml/2 tbsp olive oil
1 large onion, coarsely chopped
2 green (bell) peppers, seeded and diced
2 × 400g/14oz cans chopped tomatoes
15ml/1 tbsp fresh lime juice
10ml/2 tsp Tabasco sauce
2.5ml/½ tsp salt
30ml/2 tbsp chopped fresh coriander
   (cilantro)

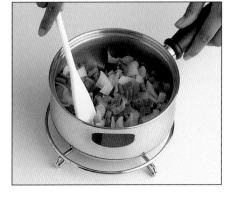

I Heat the oil in a large, heavy pan. Add the onion and peppers and sauté for 5–6 minutes, stirring frequently.

2 Add the tomatoes, stir and bring to the boil. Reduce the heat and simmer for 6–8 minutes until the salsa thickens a bit. Remove from heat, stir in the lime juice, Tabasco sauce and salt, then cool.

3 Stir the chopped coriander leaves through the cooled salsa and pot in clean jars. Cover and refrigerate.

Cajun Bloody Mary (top) and Avery Island Salsa (bottom).

Fish & Shellfish

Louisiana is a low-lying and wet state with a long coastline along the Gulf of Mexico, so there is no shortage of fish and seafood, both from the fresh waters of the bayous and rivers and from the sea. But much of what is commonplace in fishmarkets there – oysters, soft-shell crab, redfish and crawfish – are either hugely expensive or completely unknown outside the region. With fish, however, more than with any other foodstuff, substitution is acceptable, and unless an expensive ingredient is essential to the finished dish, I have recommended cheaper and more widely available fish.

Louisiana Seafood Gumbo

Gumbo is a soup, but it is served over rice as a main course. This recipe is based on a gumbo that chef John Folse, of the renowned Louisiana restaurant Lafitte's Landing, served on a visit to London. In his neck of the bayous, where they are cheap and prolific, oysters are an important ingredient. However, his suggestion to substitute mussels for oysters works very well too.

SERVES 6

INGREDIENTS
450g/1lb mussels
450g/1lb prawns (shrimp)
1 cooked crab weighing about 1kg/2¼lb
salt
1 small bunch of parsley, leaves chopped and stalks reserved
150ml/5fl oz/⅔ cup cooking oil
115g/4oz/1 cup plain (all-purpose) flour
1 green (bell) pepper, seeded and chopped
1 large onion, chopped
2 celery sticks, sliced
3 garlic cloves, finely chopped
75g/3oz smoked spiced sausage, skinned and sliced
6 spring onions (scallions), shredded
cayenne pepper
Tabasco sauce
boiled American long-grain rice, to serve

1 Wash the mussels in several changes of cold water, scrubbing away any barnacles and pulling off the black 'beards' that protrude between the shells. Discard any mussels that are broken or any open ones that do not close when tapped firmly.

2 Heat 250ml/8fl oz/1 cup water in a deep pan and, when it boils, add the mussels. Cover tightly and cook over a high heat, shaking often, for 3 minutes. As the mussels open, lift them out with tongs into a sieve (strainer) set over a bowl. Discard any that do not open after a further 1 minute of cooking.

3 Shell the mussels, discarding the shells. Return the liquor from the bowl to the pan and make the quantity up to 2 litres/3½ pints/9 cups with water.

4 Shell the prawns and put the shells and heads into the pan.

5 Remove all the meat from the crab (*see* the recipe for Corn and Crab Bisque), separating the brown and white meat. Add all the pieces of shell to the pan with 10ml/2 tsp salt.

6 Bring the shellfish stock to the boil, skimming regularly to remove the froth that rises as boiling point approaches.

7 When no more froth rises from the shellfish stock, add the parsley stalks and simmer for 15 minutes. Cool the stock, then strain off the liquor, discarding all the solids. Make up to 2 litres/3½ pints/9 cups with water.

8 Make a roux with the oil and flour (*see* Introduction). Stir constantly over the heat with a wooden spoon or whisk until it reaches a golden-brown colour. It is vital to stir constantly, to darken the roux without burning. Should black specks occur at any stage of cooking, discard the roux and start again.

9 As soon as the roux is golden-brown, add the pepper, onion, celery and garlic and continue cooking until they are soft – about 3 minutes. Then add the sausage. Reheat the stock.

10 Stir the brown crabmeat into the roux, then ladle in the hot stock a little at a time, stirring constantly until the stock is all smoothly incorporated. Bring to a low boil and simmer the soup for 30 minutes, partially covered.

11 Add the prawns, mussels, white crabmeat and spring onions. Return to the boil, season with salt if necessary, cayenne pepper and a dash or two of Tabasco sauce, and simmer for a further minute.

12 Add the chopped parsley leaves and serve immediately, ladling the soup over the hot rice spooned into soup plates.

COOK'S TIP

It is important to have the onion, green pepper and celery prepared and ready to add to the roux the minute it reaches the correct golden-brown stage, as this arrests its darkening.

Blackened Redfish

Paul Prudhomme, inventor of this dish, recommends it be cooked out of doors over a butane flame. Since this is not practical for most cooks, there are a few precautions to be taken for more conventional cooking.

First, do not attempt this dish in a kitchen you cannot ventilate, for this fierce cooking method produces plenty of smoke: open the windows, turn on extractor fans – and warn close neighbours!

You must have a really heavy cast-iron frying pan with a flat base – ridged ones hold the butter in the furrows, where it burns. Be brave about heating the pan over a high flame until it develops a greyish-white smoky patina before you put the fish in.

Wear an apron: you would not catch Chef Prudhomme blackening his redfish without his kitchen whites. Also, tackle the recipe by making it for just two at first, at least until you know what to expect. It makes the fastest possible supper dish for a couple.

SERVES 2

INGREDIENTS
*2 fillets of redfish or red snapper,
    not less than 2cm/³⁄₄in thick*
75g/3oz/6 tbsp butter
5ml/1 tsp paprika
2.5ml/½ tsp dried oregano
1.5ml/¼ tsp salt
*good pinch each of garlic salt and
    cayenne pepper*
a good grinding of black pepper
*lime or lemon wedges and mixed salad,
    to serve*

1 Make sure that the fillets are thoroughly defrosted if you bought them frozen. Pat them dry with kitchen paper and put them on a plate.

2 In a small pan, melt the butter and swirl in all the seasonings. Pour over the fish and turn the fish in the butter to keep it coated on both sides until you are ready to cook.

3 Put a heavy frying pan over a medium-high heat and leave it there for 5 minutes. It will smoke and slowly develop a grey-white patina.

4 Turn the fillets once more in the butter and put them skin-side down on to the pan. Cook, pressing down regularly with a fish slice or metal spatula, for 2 minutes or until the skin is crisp and very dark.

5 Pour a little of the seasoned butter over the top of each fillet and turn them over. Cook for a further 2 minutes or so, again pressing down with the fish slice, until the fish is cooked through.

6 Serve the fillets on hot plates, with the remaining seasoned butter poured over, and garnished with lime or lemon wedges and accompanied by a mixed salad.

COOK'S TIP

A soft vegetable goes well with Blackened Redfish – Maque Choux or Smothered Okra, plus perhaps a Potato Salad.

VARIATION

The same method, and the same spiced butter, works well with a skinned chicken breast opened out with a series of small 'butterfly' cuts and beaten flat between 2 sheets of clear film (plastic wrap). However, the average frying pan will take just one at a time – so when you are cooking the redfish, make a little extra of the spiced butter and keep some for a solitary supper treat on another occasion. Cook the chicken for about 3 minutes each side.

Fried Fish with Tartare Sauce and Hush Puppies

The story goes that fishermen frying their catch used to drop pieces of stiffened batter into the fat to fry. They would then throw the fried batter to their dogs to hush their hungry howlings – hence the name of hush puppies, a traditional Southern food.

SERVES 4

INGREDIENTS

For the tartare sauce
150ml/5fl oz/²⁄₃ cup mayonnaise
15ml/1 tbsp chopped dill pickles
5 pitted green olives, chopped
2 spring onions (scallions), finely shredded
15ml/1 tbsp lemon juice
1–2 dashes Tabasco sauce

For the hush puppies
115g/4oz/1 cup cornmeal
50g/2oz/½ cup plain (all-purpose) flour
7.5ml/1½ tsp baking powder
1 garlic clove, crushed with 1 tsp salt
2 spring onions (scallions), finely shredded
1 egg, lightly beaten
about 75ml/5 tbsp milk
25g/1oz/2 tbsp butter

For the fish coating
25g/1oz/¼ cup plain (all-purpose) flour
25g/1oz/¼ cup cornflour (cornstarch)
50g/2oz/½ cup cornmeal
2.5ml/½ tsp dried oregano
2.5ml/½ tsp dried thyme
5ml/1 tsp salt
5ml/1 tsp cayenne pepper
5ml/1 tsp paprika
10ml/2 tsp dry mustard powder
1 egg
about 120ml/4fl oz/½ cup milk

For the fish fillets
oil, for deep-frying
4 skinned plaice fillets, thawed if frozen
lemon slices and fresh parsley sprigs,
*　to garnish*

｜ Mix all the ingredients for the tartare sauce and set aside.

2 Next make the hush puppy batter. Mix the cornmeal, flour and baking powder and stir in the crushed garlic and spring onions. Stir in the egg with a fork.

3 Heat 5 tbsp milk and the butter together slowly until the butter melts, then raise the heat and, when it boils, stir thoroughly into the dry ingredients, adding a little more milk if necessary to make a stiff dough. Leave to cool.

4 To make the fish coating, mix the flours, all the herbs and seasonings for the fish coating in a shallow dish. Beat the egg and milk together lightly in another shallow dish.

5 Scoop out pieces of hush puppy batter no bigger than a walnut and roll into balls between wetted hands.

6 Heat the oil for deep-frying. Fry the hush puppies in batches, turning them until they are deep golden-brown all over.

7 The hush puppies will swell in cooking, and they need to be cooked through to the middle, so do not have the oil fiercely hot to start with. It should sizzle and froth up round them as you drop them in, but not brown them immediately. Lift out the hush puppies as they are done with a slotted spoon and drain on kitchen paper. Keep warm.

8 Coat the fish fillets, dipping each fillet first in the egg mixture and then in the cornmeal mixture.

9 Fry the fillets two at a time for 2–3 minutes on each side, until crisp and golden brown. Drain on kitchen paper and serve with the hush puppies, garnished with lemon slices and sprigs of parsley.

COOK'S TIP

Louisiana cooks use a specially fine-ground cornmeal in their coating mixture. The nearest widely available substitute is masa harina, *from which Mexican cooks make tortillas. It is available from specialist shops or by mail order from The Cool Chile Co. (see their website www.coolchile.co.uk for details).*

Salmon Court-bouillon

This dish typifies the difference between classical French cuisine and the frugal Creole: French cooks discard the flavouring vegetables from the cooking liquor, while in Louisiana all the goodness is kept in the pot and enriched with a dark roux that is the signature of the local cuisine.

Redfish is the Creole choice for the court-bouillon treatment because it is firm-textured, plentiful and cheap. Farmed salmon is equally abundant in other areas and makes a good alternative. Long-grain rice or pasta makes a good accompaniment.

SERVES 6

INGREDIENTS
6 salmon steaks
2 medium onions
4 celery sticks
3 bay leaves
*6 sprigs fresh parsley, leaves chopped and
    stalks reserved*
400g/14oz can tomatoes
175ml/6fl oz/¾ cup cooking oil
115g/4oz/1 cup plain (all-purpose) flour
1 large green (bell) pepper, chopped
2 garlic cloves, chopped
115g/4oz mushrooms, sliced
5ml/1 tsp dried thyme
5ml/1 tsp dried basil
salt and freshly ground black pepper
6 spring onions (scallions), shredded
*½ lemon, thinly sliced, plus lemon wedges
    to serve*

1 When you buy the salmon steaks, ask the fishmonger for salmon trimmings for the stock. Put these trimmings into a deep pan or flameproof casserole with 2 litres/3½ pints/9 cups cold water.

2 Peel the onions, keeping the skins. Chop 1½ onions and put the remaining half with the onion skins into the pan with the salmon trimmings. Break one celery stick into three pieces and add to the stock with one of the bay leaves.

3 Bring to the boil, skimming off the froth as it rises. When no further froth rises, add the reserved parsley stalks with some salt. Simmer for 15 minutes, then strain, discarding the solids.

4 Thinly slice the remaining celery sticks. Chop the canned tomatoes on a plate, keeping all the liquor.

5 In a large pan or flameproof casserole, make a roux with the oil and flour (*see* Introduction). It should be nutty brown, a stage darker than that in the Louisiana Seafood Gumbo recipe.

6 The minute the roux reaches the right stage of nutty brown, add the chopped onions, green pepper, garlic, the remaining celery and mushrooms, and cook for a further 3 minutes.

7 Remove the roux from the heat while you reheat the fish stock. Return the roux to the heat and stir in the fish stock a little at a time. Add the chopped tomatoes, remaining 2 bay leaves, the thyme and basil, bring to a low boil, then simmer for 30 minutes. Check the seasoning and correct with salt and black pepper.

8 Put the salmon steaks into the stock with the lemon slices and spring onions. Cook for 5–6 minutes, or until the fish is just done. Serve hot, garnished with the chopped parsley leaves and lemon wedges.

Cod Steaks with Dill-Mustard Sauce

Catfish is the preferred Deep South choice of a firm white fish. Cod is a good alternative if you are unable to buy catfish. Here it is fried to a light golden crust in butter and served with a pungent mustard sauce.

SERVES 4

INGREDIENTS
For the sauce
30ml/2 tbsp Dijon mustard
150ml/5fl oz/⅔ cup mayonnaise
30ml/2 tbsp finely chopped fresh dill

For the cod steaks
30ml/2 tbsp milk
4 cod steaks
30ml/2 tbsp plain (all-purpose) flour
10ml/2 tsp dry mustard powder
salt and freshly ground black pepper
50g/2oz/4 tbsp butter
lemon wedges and fresh dill sprigs,
   to garnish

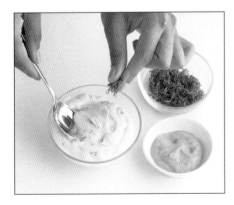

1 First mix all the ingredients for the sauce and set aside.

2 Put the milk in a soup plate and lay the cod steaks in it. On a separate plate, mix the flour, mustard powder, salt and pepper.

3 Melt the butter in a frying pan. Turn the cod in the milk and dip immediately in the dry coating mixture, then shake off any excess flour.

4 When the butter sizzles, fry the cod steaks for 2–3 minutes on each side until the outside is crisp and pale golden, and you can just pull the flesh from the bone with the sharp tip of a knife.

5 Serve hot from the pan, garnished with lemon wedges and sprigs of dill. Pass the sauce at the table.

COOK'S TIP

The two varieties of mustard in this recipe serve rather different functions. Mustard powder, though initially hotter, loses its heat in cooking and serves to add resonant depth of flavour and golden crispness to the coating. The Dijon in the sauce is a mellower flavour to begin with, but loses none of its flavour through cooking and contributes pungency to the sauce, which should be served at room temperature. Accompany the dish with a steamed crisp green vegetable such as mangetouts (snow peas) or runner or French (green) beans.

Shrimp Creole

As sure as the Mississippi flows into the Gulf of Mexico, there will be Shrimp Creole on the Friday lunch tables of Louisiana. This is a modernized, more 'haute Creole' version, based on that served at the Commander's Palace in the beautiful Garden District of New Orleans.

SERVES 6–8

INGREDIENTS
75g/3oz/6 tbsp unsalted butter
1 large onion, halved and thinly sliced
1 large green (bell) pepper, halved, seeded and thinly sliced
2 celery sticks, thinly sliced
2 garlic cloves, thinly sliced
1 bay leaf
30ml/2 tbsp paprika
450g/1lb/2 cups skinned, chopped fresh tomatoes
250ml/8fl oz/1 cup tomato juice
20ml/4 tsp Worcestershire sauce
4–6 dashes Tabasco sauce
salt
7.5ml/1½ tsp cornflour (cornstarch)
1.5kg/3lb raw prawns (shrimp), peeled and deveined
boiled rice with an optional garnish of chopped fresh parsley and shreds of lemon peel, to serve

1 Melt 25g/1oz/2 tbsp of the butter in a wide pan and sauté the onion, green pepper, celery, garlic and bay leaf for 1–2 minutes until all are hot and coated in butter.

2 Add the paprika, tomatoes and tomato juice, stir in the Worcestershire and Tabasco sauces, bring to the boil and simmer, uncovered, to reduce the volume by about a quarter, by which time the vegetables should have softened. Season with salt to taste.

3 Mix the cornflour with 75ml/5 tbsp cold water in a dish and, swirling it around, pour it into the tomato sauce.

4 Stir the sauce constantly for a couple of minutes, then turn off the heat.

5 Sauté the prawns in batches in the remaining butter until pink and tender – this will take 2–4 minutes, depending on the size of the prawns.

6 Meanwhile, reheat the tomato sauce. When all the prawns are cooked, add them to the sauce and stir over the heat for no more than 1 minute. Check the seasoning and serve with fluffy boiled rice, garnished, if you like, with chopped fresh parsley and shreds of lemon peel.

COOK'S TIP

Pre-cooked prawns may be all that are available, in which case incorporate all the butter into the sauce-making, skip the sauté stage and add the ready-cooked prawns to the sauce when reheating it, giving them just long enough to heat through.

The sauce can be made in advance up to step 4 and refrigerated for reheating later.

Oyster and Bacon Brochettes

Six oysters per person make a good appetizer, served with the seasoned oyster liquor to trickle over the skewers. Increase the oyster ration to nine and serve hot with a cool salad as a lunch main course. You might then beat some olive oil into the sauce and use it to dress the salad.

SERVES 4–6

INGREDIENTS
36 oysters
18 rashers (strips) rindless streaky (fatty) bacon
115g/4oz/1 cup plain (all-purpose) flour
15ml/1 tbsp paprika
5ml/1 tsp cayenne pepper
5ml/1 tsp salt
5ml/1 tsp garlic salt
10ml/2 tsp dried oregano
freshly ground black pepper
oil, for shallow-frying
celery leaves and red chillies, to garnish

For the sauce
½ red chilli pepper, seeded and very finely chopped
2 spring onions (scallions), very finely chopped
30ml/2 tbsp finely chopped fresh parsley
liquor from shucking oysters
juice of ¼–½ lemon
salt and freshly ground black pepper

1 Shuck the oysters over a bowl to catch their liquor for the sauce. Wrap your left hand in a clean tea towel and cup the deep shell of each oyster in your wrapped hand. Work the point of a strong short-bladed knife into the hinge between the shells and twist.

2 Push the knife in and work it to cut the muscle, holding the shell closed. Pour the liquor from the deep shell into the bowl.

3 Cut under the flesh of the oyster to free the meat from the shell. Discard the drained shells.

4 Halve the bacon rashers across and wrap each oyster in half a rasher, then thread them on to 4 or 6 skewers.

5 Next, make the sauce. Mix the chopped chilli, spring onions and parsley into the bowl of oyster liquor, and sharpen to taste with lemon juice. Season and transfer to a small bowl.

6 Mix the flour with the paprika, cayenne pepper, salt, garlic salt, oregano and a good grinding of black pepper. Spread the mixture on a flat plate and roll the skewered oysters in it, shaking the surplus back on to the plate.

7 Heat 2.5cm/1in depth of oil in a wide frying pan and fry the skewers, in batches if necessary, over a medium-high heat, turning until they are crisp and brown all over. They should take 3–4 minutes each.

8 Drain the skewers on kitchen paper and serve with the garnish and accompanied by the little bowl of sauce.

COOK'S TIP

Individual oysters can be skewered and cooked on cocktail sticks (toothpicks) to serve hot as the smartest of canapés. Pass the sauce with them in a little bowl for dipping.

Mussel and Artichoke Casserole

New Orleans cooks use oysters and their liquor, but plump golden mussels deliver a sea-scented liquor that is just as delicious with sweet-flavoured artichoke hearts, particularly when cooked in white wine.

Serve with plenty of hot French bread as a satisfying one-pot meal, followed by a salad.

SERVES 4

INGREDIENTS
2kg/4½lb mussels
6–8 sprigs fresh parsley
2 bay leaves
120ml/4fl oz/½ cup white wine
400g/14oz can artichoke hearts
50g/2oz/4 tbsp butter
50g/2oz/½ cup plain (all-purpose) flour
salt and freshly ground black pepper
6 spring onions (scallions),
  roughly chopped
45ml/3 tbsp fresh white breadcrumbs
45ml/3 tbsp grated Parmesan cheese

I Clean the mussels (*see* Louisiana Seafood Gumbo for the method).

2 Cut the leaves from the parsley, reserving the stalks. Chop the leaves roughly and set aside. Put the stalks into a deep pan with the bay leaves and wine. Drain the artichoke hearts and set aside, keeping their liquor. Add 120ml/4fl oz/½ cup of the liquor to the pot and bring to the boil.

3 Cook the mussels in batches in the pot over a high heat, shaking the covered pot (*see* Louisiana Seafood Gumbo, for the method). Use tongs to lift the mussels as they open and place in a large sieve (strainer) set over a bowl.

4 Shell the mussels, keeping any liquor that drips through into the bowl.

5 When all the mussels are shelled, pour the liquor from the pot through the sieve, discarding the solids.

6 Quarter the artichoke hearts.

7 Reheat the strained mussel liquor. Meanwhile, preheat the grill (broiler) and position the grill shelf low.

8 In a heavy pan, make a roux with the butter and flour (*see* Introduction). As soon as it is pale golden, remove the pan from the heat and slowly begin adding the mussel liquor, a little at a time, stirring the mixture constantly.

9 Return to a gentle heat when the sauce loosens and smooths out, and continue to stir in liquor a little at a time. Simmer to a creamy sauce. Check the seasoning. Heat the grill (broiler) to high.

10 Stir the mussels, artichoke hearts, spring onions and most of the chopped parsley leaves gently into the sauce and pour into a flameproof dish.

11 Mix the breadcrumbs and Parmesan and sprinkle evenly over the dish. Grill (broil), watching constantly, until the top is golden. Garnish with the remaining chopped parsley leaves and serve immediately from the dish.

Trout Meunière with Pecan Butter

The Louisiana version of the French dish, trout with almonds.

SERVES 4

INGREDIENTS
For the pecan butter
50g/2oz/½ cup shelled pecan halves
50g/2oz/4 tbsp unsalted butter
10ml/2 tsp Worcestershire sauce
5ml/1 tsp lemon juice

For the trout fillets
4 large fillets of trout
10ml/2 tsp paprika
5ml/1 tsp cayenne pepper
5ml/1 tsp dried oregano
a pinch of dried thyme
2.5ml/½ tsp garlic salt
5ml/1 tsp salt
freshly ground black pepper
1 egg
120ml/4fl oz/½ cup milk
45ml/3 tbsp plain (all-purpose) flour
oil, for shallow-frying

1 First, make the pecan butter. Preheat the oven to 180°C/350°F/ Gas 4. Spread the pecans on a baking sheet and roast in the oven for 15–20 minutes. Set aside to cool.

2 Whizz the roasted pecans in bursts in a food processor or blender to chop them quite finely. Add the butter, Worcestershire sauce and lemon juice, and blend the mixture thoroughly.

3 Scrape out the pecan butter on to clear film (plastic wrap), roll into a column, wrap and chill until required.

4 Rinse the trout fillets under the cold tap, then dry. Remove any remaining bones.

5 In a small bowl, mix the paprika, cayenne pepper, oregano, thyme, garlic salt, salt and a good grinding of black pepper. Sprinkle a pinch or two of the mixture over each fillet.

6 Lightly beat the egg and milk together in a shallow dish and beat in 5ml/1 tsp of the seasoning mix.

7 In another shallow dish, combine the remaining seasoning mix thoroughly with the flour.

8 Heat the oil for shallow-frying in a deep frying pan.

9 Pass the trout fillets through the egg-wash mixture, then through the seasoned flour, shaking off any excess. Fry until golden, then drain them on kitchen paper and keep warm.

10 Unwrap the chilled butter and cut into coin-thick slices.

11 Serve the fillets with a slice of pecan butter on top of each one.

Meat, Poultry
& Game

*Game was of primary importance to the early
settlers in Louisiana, both for Cajuns, who
hunted for their own food, and Creoles, who had
it caught and cooked for their tables. Now, on a
day-to-day basis, domesticated chicken, duck and
poussin and farmed quail replace the feathered
wild game that once formed the main source of
meat. Louisiana natives are also keen on pork:
the pig was introduced to America by the
first settlers from Europe.*

Chicken and Prawn Jambalaya

The mixture of chicken, seafood and rice suggests a close relationship to the Spanish paella, but the name is more probably derived from 'jambon' (the French for ham), 'à la ya' (Creole for rice). Jambalayas are a colourful mixture of highly flavoured ingredients, and are always made in large quantities for big family or celebration meals.

SERVES 10

INGREDIENTS
2 × 1.5kg/3lb chicken
salt and freshly ground black pepper
450g/1lb piece raw smoked gammon
    (smoked or cured ham)
50g/2oz/4 tbsp lard or bacon fat
50g/2oz/½ cup plain (all-purpose) flour
3 medium onions, finely sliced
2 green (bell) peppers, seeded and sliced
675g/1½lb tomatoes, skinned
    and chopped
2–3 garlic cloves, crushed
10ml/2 tsp chopped fresh thyme or
    5ml/1 tsp dried thyme
24 Mediterranean prawns (large shrimp),
    beheaded and peeled
500g/1¼lb/3 cups American long-grain
    rice
2–3 dashes Tabasco sauce
1 bunch spring onions (scallions), finely
    chopped (including the green parts)
45ml/3 tbsp chopped fresh parsley

1 Cut each chicken into 10 pieces and season with salt and pepper.

2 Dice the gammon, discarding the rind and fat.

3 In a large heavy pan or flameproof casserole, melt the lard or bacon fat. Add the chicken pieces and brown them all over, lifting them out with a slotted spoon and setting them aside as they are done.

4 Turn the heat down, sprinkle the flour on to the fat in the pan and stir constantly until the roux turns light golden-brown (*see* Introduction).

5 Return the chicken pieces to the pan, add the diced gammon, onions, green peppers, tomatoes, garlic and thyme and cook, stirring regularly, for 10 minutes, then stir in the prawns.

6 Stir the rice into the pan with one and a half times the rice's volume in cold water. Season with salt, pepper and Tabasco sauce. Bring to the boil and cook over a gentle heat until the rice is tender and the liquid has been absorbed. Add a little extra boiling water if the rice looks likely to dry out before it is cooked.

7 Mix the spring onions and parsley into the finished dish, reserving a little of the mixture to sprinkle over the jambalaya. Serve hot.

COOK'S TIP

The roux thickening is a vital part of Cajun cooking, and is particularly essential to making jambalaya. Cook the roux over a low heat, watching closely to make sure it does not develop dark flecks, which indicate burning. Do not stop stirring for an instant.

Duck Breasts with Red Pepper Jelly Glaze
and Grilled Sweet Potatoes

Sweet potatoes have pinkish skins and flesh varying from creamy white to deep orange. Choose a long cylindrically-shaped tuber for the neatest discs.

SERVES 2

INGREDIENTS

2 duck breast fillets
coarse sea salt and freshly ground
    black pepper
1 pink-skinned sweet potato weighing
    about 400g/14oz
30ml/2 tbsp Red Pepper Jelly
    (see page 28)
15ml/1 tbsp sherry vinegar
50g/2oz/4 tbsp butter, melted
green salad, to serve

1 Slash the skin of the duck breasts diagonally at 2.5cm/1in intervals, then rub salt and pepper over the skin and into the cuts.

2 Preheat the grill (broiler) with the shelf set so that the meat will be 7.5–10cm/3–4in from the heat.

3 Scrub the sweet potato and cut into 1cm/½in thick slices, discarding the rounded ends.

4 Grill (broil) the meat, skin-side up first, for 5 minutes, then flesh-side up for 8–10 minutes, according to how pink you like your duck.

5 Meanwhile, warm the jelly and vinegar together in a bowl set in a pan of hot water, stirring to mix them as the jelly melts.

COOK'S TIP

Pork chops are also good grilled and caramelized with the jelly, and the grilled sweet potatoes are excellent with them. Sweet potatoes also go well with grilled gammon steaks (smoked or cured ham) for a quick supper.

6 Remove the grill (broiling) pan from the heat, turn the duck breasts skin-side up and paint with the jelly mixture. Return to the grill and cook for a further 2–3 minutes until the glaze caramelizes. Transfer the duck breasts to a serving plate and keep warm.

7 Brush the sweet potato slices with melted butter and arrange in the grill pan. Sprinkle with coarse sea salt and place one level higher under the grill than the duck breasts were.

8 Cook the sweet potatoes under the grill for 4–5 minutes on each side until soft, brushing with more butter and sprinkling with sea salt and black pepper when you turn them.

9 Serve the duck breasts sliced, with the sweet potatoes and a green salad.

Smothered Rabbit

Game has always formed a big part of the Cajun diet – it was the only meat available to the early settlers. The smothering technique gives plenty of flavour to a domestic rabbit, too. Ask your butcher or game dealer to prepare the rabbit pieces for you.

SERVES 4

INGREDIENTS
1 rabbit, skinned, cleaned and cut into
*   8 pieces*
10ml/2 tsp salt
2.5ml/½ tsp garlic salt
2.5ml/½ tsp dried oregano
good pinch each of freshly ground black
*   pepper and cayenne pepper*
50g/2oz/½ cup plain (all-purpose) flour
60ml/4 tbsp cooking oil
1 medium onion, chopped
1 celery stick, chopped
1 large garlic clove, crushed
1 bay leaf
350ml/12fl oz/1½ cups chicken stock
3 spring onions (scallions), shredded
30ml/2 tbsp chopped fresh parsley
cooked mangetouts (snow peas), to serve

1 Mix the salt, garlic salt, oregano, black pepper and cayenne pepper together. Sprinkle the rabbit pieces lightly, using about half the seasoning mix, and pat it in with your fingers.

2 Put the rest of the seasoning mix together with the flour into a polythene bag, shake to mix, then shake the pieces of rabbit in this to dredge them, shaking the surplus back into the bag as you lift them out. Reserve the remaining seasoned flour.

3 Heat the oil in a heavy flameproof casserole and fry the rabbit pieces until browned on all sides. Do this in batches so as not to crowd the pan, removing each one as it is ready.

4 When all the rabbit is browned, cook the onion and celery in the same pan for 5 minutes, stirring regularly. Add the garlic and bay leaf.

5 Heat the stock. Meanwhile, add 1 tbsp of the reserved seasoned flour to the oil in the pan and stir over the heat for 1 minute. Remove from the heat and gradually stir in some of the hot stock. When the sauce loosens, return the pan to the heat and add the remaining stock, stirring constantly until boiling point is reached.

6 Lower the heat, return the browned rabbit pieces to the casserole, cover and simmer for about 1 hour, until the rabbit is very tender.

7 Check the seasoning and stir in the spring onions and parsley. Serve with mangetouts and perhaps some crusty bread.

COOK'S TIP

You could make Smothered Chicken in exactly the same way with 4 chicken pieces.

Chicken Sauce Piquante

Sauce Piquante goes with everything that runs, flies or swims in Louisiana – you will even find Alligator Sauce Piquante on menus. It is based on the brown Cajun roux and has chilli peppers to give it heat: vary the heat by altering the number you use.

SERVES 4

INGREDIENTS

4 chicken legs or 2 legs and 2 breasts
75ml/5 tbsp cooking oil
50g/2oz/½ cup plain (all-purpose) flour
1 medium onion, chopped
2 celery sticks, sliced
1 green (bell) pepper, seeded and diced
2 garlic cloves, crushed
1 bay leaf
2.5ml/½ tsp dried thyme
2.5ml/½ tsp dried oregano
1–2 red chilli peppers, seeded and
  finely chopped
400g/14oz can tomatoes, chopped, with
  their juice
300ml/10fl oz/1¼ cups chicken stock
salt and freshly ground black pepper
watercress or rocket (arugula), to garnish
boiled potatoes, to serve

1 Halve the chicken legs through the joint, or the breasts across the middle, to give 8 pieces.

2 In a heavy frying pan, fry the chicken pieces in the oil until brown on all sides, lifting them out and setting them aside as they are done.

3 Strain the oil from the pan into a heavy flameproof casserole. Heat it and stir in the flour. Stir constantly over a low heat until the roux is the colour of peanut butter (*see* Introduction).

4 Immediately the roux reaches the right colour, add the onion, celery and green pepper to the pan and stir over the heat for 2–3 minutes.

5 Add the garlic, bay leaf, thyme, oregano and chilli peppers as preferred. Stir for 1 minute, then turn down the heat and stir in the tomatoes with their juice.

6 Return the casserole to the heat and gradually stir in the stock. Add the browned chicken pieces, cover and leave to simmer for 45 minutes, until the chicken is tender.

7 If there is too much sauce or the mixture is too runny, remove the lid for the last 10–15 minutes of the cooking time and raise the heat a little.

8 Check the seasoning and serve, garnished with watercress or rocket and accompanied by boiled potatoes, or perhaps rice or pasta, and a green vegetable or salad of your choice.

COOK'S TIP

If you prefer to err on the side of caution with chilli heat, use just 1 chilli pepper and hot up the seasoning at the end with a dash or two of Tabasco sauce.

  The oil in chilli peppers clings to your skin and could hurt if you then rub your eyes. Always scrape out the seeds under running cold water and wash your hands carefully after handling chillies.

Poussins with Dirty Rice

This traditional rice dish is called 'dirty' not because of the bits in it (though the roux and chicken livers do discolour it) but because one nickname for jazz is 'dirty music', and the rice here is certainly jazzed up.

SERVES 4

INGREDIENTS
For the rice
4 tbsp cooking oil
25g/1oz/¼ cup plain (all-purpose) flour
50g/2oz/4 tbsp butter
1 large onion, chopped
2 celery sticks, chopped
1 green (bell) pepper, seeded and diced
2 garlic cloves, crushed
200g/7oz minced (ground) pork
225g/8oz chicken livers, trimmed and sliced
salt, freshly ground black pepper and Tabasco sauce
300ml/10fl oz/1¼ cups chicken stock
4 spring onions (scallions), shredded
45ml/3 tbsp chopped fresh parsley
225g/8oz/generous 1 cup American long-grain rice, cooked

For the birds
4 poussins
2 bay leaves, halved
25g/1oz/2 tbsp butter
salt and freshly ground black pepper
1 lemon, for squeezing

1 In a small heavy pan, make a roux with 2 tbsp of the oil and the flour (*see* Introduction). When it is a chestnut-brown colour, remove the pan from the heat and place it immediately on a cold surface.

2 Heat the remaining 2 tbsp oil with the butter in a frying pan and stir-fry the onion, celery and green pepper for about 5 minutes.

3 Add the garlic and pork and stir-fry for 5 minutes, breaking up the pork and stirring to cook it evenly.

4 Add the chicken livers and fry for 2–3 minutes until they have changed colour all over. Season with salt, pepper and a dash of Tabasco sauce.

5 Stir the roux into the stir-fried mixture, then gradually add in the stock. When the mixture begins to bubble, cover and cook for 30 minutes, stirring occasionally. Then uncover and cook for a further 15 minutes, stirring frequently.

6 Preheat the oven to 200°C/400°F/ Gas 6. Mix the spring onions and parsley into the meat mixture and stir it all into the cooked rice.

7 Put ½ bay leaf and 15ml/1 tbsp rice into each poussin. Rub the outside with the butter and season with salt and pepper.

8 Put the birds on a rack in a roasting pan, squeeze the juice from the lemon over them, then roast them in the oven for 35–40 minutes, basting twice with the pan juices.

9 Put the remaining rice into a shallow ovenproof dish, cover it and place on a low shelf in the oven for the last 15–20 minutes of the birds' cooking time.

10 Serve the birds on a bed of dirty rice with the roasting pan juices (drained of fat) poured over.

COOK'S TIP

You can substitute quails for the poussins, in which case offer two per person and stuff each little bird with 2 tsp of the dirty rice before roasting for about 20 minutes.

Pork Chops with Lemon and Garlic Grilling Sauce

Another recipe from the McIlhenny family, producers of Tabasco sauce. They like their food on the hot side: cautious cooks can start off with less Tabasco in the mixture, adding a dash or two more at the end to get it right.

SERVES 4

INGREDIENTS
4 pork chops
115g/4oz/½ cup butter
½ lemon
1 tbsp Worcestershire sauce
7.5ml/1½ tsp Tabasco sauce
1 garlic clove, finely chopped
salt and freshly ground black pepper
grilled (bell) peppers and tomatoes,
*   to serve*

I Preheat the grill (broiler). Arrange the chops in the grill (broiling) pan, but do not place them under the grill.

2 Melt the butter in a small non-aluminium pan. Squeeze in the juice of the lemon and bring to simmering point.

3 Add the Worcestershire and Tabasco sauces and the garlic to the pan, and continue cooking over a low heat, without allowing the garlic to brown, for 5 minutes or so. Season to taste with salt and pepper.

4 Brush the tops of the chops liberally with the sauce, place the pan under the grill and grill (broil) until they begin to brown – about 5 minutes.

5 Turn the chops and brush with more sauce. Grill for a further 5 minutes or so, depending on the thickness of the chops. You can trickle a little more of the sauce over to serve. Accompany the chops with grilled peppers and tomatoes.

COOK'S TIP

This makes a very good sauce for cooking on the barbecue as well as for indoor grilling. On the barbecue it complements most vegetables, particularly the fashionable Mediterranean ones such as courgettes (zucchini), aubergine (eggplant) and red or green (bell) peppers. Served either as a vegetarian dish with rice or as an accompaniment to barbecued meat or fish, you could assemble such vegetables in chunks on skewers and baste with the sauce while turning over the coals.

Under the grill, the sauce is just as good with chicken pieces, duck breasts or lamb steaks as it is with pork.

Roast Pork with Cajun Stuffing

The familiar trinity of onion, celery and green pepper gives Cajun flavour to a handsome roast, complete with crackling.

SERVES 6

INGREDIENTS

1.5kg/3½lb boned loin of pork
15ml/1 tbsp salt
5ml/1 tsp each freshly ground black
*   pepper, paprika, cayenne pepper*
*   and dried oregano*
30ml/2 tbsp cooking oil or 25g/1oz/2 tbsp
*   lard or white cooking fat*
1 small onion, finely chopped
1 celery stick, finely chopped
½ green (bell) pepper, seeded and
*   finely chopped*
1 garlic clove, crushed

1 If the pork is already tied up, then untie it. Score the pork skin closely to make good crackling (you can ask your butcher to do this). Rub 10ml/2 tsp of the salt into the skin the night before if you can; or, if not, as far in advance of cooking as possible on the day. If the meat has been refrigerated overnight, let it stand in an airy place at room temperature for a couple of hours or so before cooking.

2 Preheat the oven to 220°C/425°F/Gas 7. Mix the black pepper, paprika, cayenne pepper and oregano with the remaining 5ml/1 tsp salt, and rub over the meaty side of the meat.

3 Heat the oil or lard and gently fry the onion, celery and green pepper for 5 minutes, adding the garlic for the last minute of cooking.

4 Spread the vegetables over the inside of the meat.

5 Roll up the meat skin-side out and tie in several places.

6 Roast the meat on a rack in a roasting pan. After 30 minutes, reduce the heat to 180°C/350°F/Gas 4. Baste with the pan juices after 15 minutes and again every 20 minutes or so.

7 The overall roasting time is about 2 hours. If the crackling does not go crisp and bubbly in the latter stages, raise the oven heat a little for the last 20–30 minutes.

8 Allow the meat to rest in a warm place for 10–15 minutes before carving.

COOK'S TIP

You can roast potatoes or sweet potatoes in the pan with the meat, or bake them in their skins alongside the meat in the oven. Skim some of the fat from the pan juice and bubble the remainder with some red wine and a bay leaf to make a tasty gravy.

Pan-fried Veal with Fettuccine

This old Creole dish demonstrates obvious European antecedents.

SERVES 4

INGREDIENTS
4 thin-cut escalopes of veal, each weighing
   about 100g/3½oz
salt, freshly ground black pepper and
   cayenne pepper
2 eggs
120ml/l4fl oz/½ cup milk
30ml/2 tbsp finely grated Parmesan cheese
50g/2oz/½ cup plain (all-purpose) flour
115g/4oz/1 cup breadcrumbs
50g/2oz/4 tbsp butter
30ml/2 tbsp cooking oil
green salad, to serve

For the fettucine
salt
225g/8oz dried or 350g/12oz fresh
   fettucine
50g/2oz/4 tbsp butter
45ml/3 tbsp finely chopped fresh parsley
   (optional)
freshly ground black pepper and
   cayenne pepper

1 Sandwich each veal escalope between 2 sheets of clear film (plastic wrap) and beat out flat with a rolling pin or the flat side of a meat cleaver. Season the veal with salt, black pepper and cayenne.

2 Beat the eggs lightly with the milk and grated Parmesan in a shallow dish. Spread the flour and the breadcrumbs on separate plates.

3 Bring a large pan of salted water to the boil for the pasta. Meanwhile, melt half the butter in half the oil in a heavy frying pan.

4 You will have to cook the veal escalopes one at a time, so prepare each one as you go. Dredge it lightly with flour by turning it in the plate of flour and shaking off the excess.

5 Pass the escalope through the egg-wash, allowing the excess to drip briefly back into the dish.

6 Turn the escalope in the breadcrumbs, then drop immediately into the frying pan and cook for 2 minutes on each side. Drain on kitchen paper and keep warm. Cook the remaining escalopes in the same way, adding more butter and oil to the pan as necessary.

7 Meanwhile, cook the fettuccine: fresh pasta will take only 2–3 minutes, dried pasta up to 10 minutes.

8 When the pasta is tender but still has some firmness of bite, drain the fettucine thoroughly, return to the pan and drop in the butter.

9 When the butter melts, toss this and the parsley (if you are using it) through the pasta and spoon into a warm serving bowl. Add a little black pepper and a sprinkling of cayenne pepper.

10 Serve the veal with the fettuccine and a green salad.

COOK'S TIP

The escalopes could be cut from a turkey breast if you prefer.

Vegetables

*Cajuns love all the sweet-tasting vegetables –
corn, sweet potatoes, sweet root vegetables, such
as parsnips, and, of course, sweet peppers. Green
pepper, celery and onion are affectionately called
the 'Holy Trinity', and together they form the
cornerstone of Cajun culinary tradition. Some
vegetables are particularly valued for their soft,
melting texture. This fondness for succulence can
lead to what, to outsiders, seems an over-cooking
of vegetables, and some recipes have been
modified to suit modern tastes that prefer an
element of crispness, particularly in green
vegetables such as cabbage. Salads are also a big
feature of the Louisiana table, usually large,
hearty and hotly spiced with mustard and
cayenne pepper or Tabasco sauce.*

Vinegared Chilli Cabbage

SERVES 4–6

INGREDIENTS

*1 fresh red chilli pepper, halved, seeded
    and shredded*
*25g/1oz/2 tbsp lard, white cooking fat
    or butter*
2 garlic cloves, crushed (optional)
1 white cabbage, cored and shredded
salt
10ml/2 tsp cider vinegar
5ml/1 tsp cayenne pepper

1 Put the chilli with the lard, white
cooking fat or butter into a large pan,
and cook over medium heat until the
chilli sizzles and curls at the edges.

COOK'S TIP

*A wok with a domed lid is ideal for this
part-frying, part-steaming method of
cooking cabbage.*

2 Add the garlic and cabbage and stir,
over the heat, until the cabbage is
thoroughly coated and warm. Add salt
to taste and 75ml/5 tbsp water. Bring to
the boil, cover and lower the heat.

3 Cook, shaking the pan regularly,
for 3–4 minutes until the cabbage
wilts. Remove the lid, raise the heat
and cook off the liquid. Check the
seasoning and add more salt if
necessary. Sprinkle with vinegar and
cayenne pepper.

Coleslaw in Triple-Hot Dressing

*The triple hotness is supplied by
mustard, horseradish and Tabasco.*

SERVES 6

INGREDIENTS

½ white cabbage, cored and shredded
2 celery sticks, finely sliced
*1 green (bell) pepper, seeded and finely
    sliced*
4 spring onions (scallions), shredded
30ml/2 tbsp chopped fresh dill
cayenne pepper

For the dressing
15ml/1 tbsp Dijon mustard
10ml/2 tsp creamed horseradish
5ml/1 tsp Tabasco sauce
30ml/2 tbsp red wine vinegar
75ml/5 tbsp olive oil
salt and freshly ground black pepper

1 Combine the cabbage, celery, green
pepper and spring onions in a large
salad bowl.

2 Make the dressing. In a small bowl,
mix the mustard, horseradish and
Tabasco sauce, then gradually stir in
the vinegar with a fork and finally beat
in the olive oil and seasoning. Toss the
salad in the dressing and leave to stand,
if possible, for at least an hour. During
this time, toss the salad once or twice
in its dressing.

3 Immediately before serving, season
the salad if necessary, toss again and
sprinkle with dill and cayenne pepper.

COOK'S TIP

*This is a good salad for a buffet table or
picnic as it improves with some standing
in its dressing (or overnight in the
refrigerator) and travels well in a covered
plastic bowl or box.*

*Vinegared Chilli Cabbage (top) and
Coleslaw in Triple-Hot Dressing (bottom).*

Potato Salad

This classic dish is served not just with cold meats or grills, but as an essential side dish to a bowl of gumbo.

SERVES 6–8

INGREDIENTS
8 medium waxy potatoes
1 green (bell) pepper, seeded and diced
1 large pickled gherkin, chopped
4 spring onions (scallions), shredded
3 hard-boiled eggs, shelled and chopped
250ml/8fl oz/1 cup mayonnaise
15ml/1 tbsp Dijon mustard
salt and freshly ground black pepper
Tabasco sauce
cayenne pepper

1 Wash the potatoes and cook them in their skins in salted water. Drain when tender, and when the potatoes are cool enough, skin them and dice coarsely.

2 Mix the potatoes in a salad bowl with the green pepper, gherkin, spring onions and hard-boiled eggs.

3 In a separate bowl, mix the mayonnaise with the mustard and season the mixture with salt, black pepper and Tabasco sauce to taste.

4 Toss the dressing gently through the salad and sprinkle the top with a pinch or two of cayenne pepper.

Smothered Okra

SERVES 4–6

INGREDIENTS
500g/1¼lb okra
1 red onion, thinly sliced
25g/1oz/2 tbsp butter
1 garlic clove, crushed
4 large tomatoes, skinned, seeded and
   chopped
5ml/1 tsp red wine vinegar
salt
freshly ground black pepper and
   cayenne pepper

1 Trim the okra, cutting the stem end of each one just level with the pod.

2 Soften the onion in the butter, stirring regularly over a low heat for 5–10 minutes. Add the garlic, stir for a further minute, then add the tomatoes, vinegar, 120ml/4fl oz/½ cup water and salt, and stew, uncovered, until it becomes a thick sauce.

3 Stir in the okra, cover and cook over a very low heat for about 25 minutes, checking halfway through and adding a little more water if it is drying out – the sauce should be rather thick. When the okra are quite soft, season to taste with black and cayenne peppers. Serve hot.

Potato Salad (top) and Smothered Okra (bottom).

Maque Choux

This Cajun classic is good with ham and chicken. Some cooks add a little sugar, but for most palates the natural sweetness of the corn is enough.

SERVES 4–6

INGREDIENTS
50g/2oz/4 tbsp butter
1 large onion, finely chopped
1 green (bell) pepper, seeded and diced
2 large tomatoes, skinned and chopped
450g/1lb/4 cups frozen corn
    kernels, thawed
120ml/4fl oz/ ½ cup milk
salt, freshly ground black pepper and
    cayenne pepper

1 Melt half the butter in a large pan and soften the onion in it, stirring regularly over a low heat for about 10 minutes until it begins to turn pale gold. Add the green pepper and stir over the heat for a further minute, then add the tomatoes and leave to cook gently while you prepare the corn.

2 Put the corn kernels and milk into a food processor or blender and process in brief bursts to break up the kernels to a porridgy consistency.

3 Stir the corn mixture thoroughly into the pan and cook, partially covered, over a low heat for 20 minutes. Stir regularly, making sure that it does not stick to the bottom. If the mixture threatens to become too dry, add a little more milk. Should it still be rather wet in the latter stages, uncover, raise the heat a little and stir constantly for the last 5 minutes.

4 Stir in the rest of the butter and season quite highly with salt, black pepper and cayenne pepper. Serve hot.

COOK'S TIP

You are aiming at a consistency rather like that of scrambled eggs and, like scrambled eggs, Maque Choux is also good with bacon and fried bread for breakfast.

Potatoes, Peppers and Shallots Roasted with Rosemary

Based on a dish which is served at the Commander's Palace, this recipe exemplifies the new, rather more elegant style of New Orleans restaurant cooking.

SERVES 4

INGREDIENTS
500g/1¼lb waxy potatoes
12 shallots
2 yellow (bell) peppers
corn oil or olive oil
2 sprigs fresh rosemary
salt and freshly ground black pepper

1 Preheat the oven to 200°C/400°F/ Gas 6. Wash the potatoes and blanch for 5 minutes in boiling water. Drain and, when they are cool enough to handle, skin them and halve lengthways.

2 Peel the shallots, allowing them to fall into their natural segments. Cut each yellow pepper lengthways into 8 strips, discarding the seeds and pith.

COOK'S TIP

They do not eat much lamb in Louisiana, but if they did, this would certainly be a fine all-in-one vegetable dish to accompany it. This is also good with roast chicken.

3 Oil a shallow ovenproof dish thoroughly with corn or olive oil (corn oil is more authentic, whereas olive oil tastes better). Assemble the potatoes and peppers attractively in alternating rows and stud with the shallots.

4 Cut the rosemary sprigs into 5cm/2in lengths and tuck among the vegetables. Season the dish generously with olive oil, salt and pepper and bake in the oven, uncovered, for 30–40 minutes until all the vegetables are tender.

Red Beans and Rice

This is the classic Monday dish in Louisiana; Monday being washday and beans not minding being left to their own devices for as long as it takes to finish the laundry. Hardly worth making in small quantities because of the long cooking time, this makes a splendid supper-party dish served with good grilled (broiled) sausages and a green salad.

SERVES 8–10

INGREDIENTS
*500g/1¼lb/3⅓ cups dried red
    kidney beans
2 bay leaves
30ml/2 tbsp oil, bacon fat, lard or white
    cooking fat
1 medium onion, chopped
2 garlic cloves, finely chopped
2 celery sticks, sliced
225g/8oz piece salt pork or raw ham
salt and freshly ground black pepper
450g/1lb/2¼ cups American
    long-grain rice
45ml/3 tbsp chopped fresh parsley*

1 Start the night before. Wash the beans thoroughly in a colander under a running cold tap, then put them into a deep bowl and fill it to the top with cold water. Leave to stand overnight.

2 Drain the beans and put them into a large pan with fresh cold water to cover generously. Bring to the boil and boil hard for 10 minutes, then drain and rinse both the beans and the pan.

3 Return the beans to the pan with the bay leaves and enough fresh cold water to cover generously. Bring to the boil, reduce the heat and simmer for 30 minutes, uncovered, topping up the water in the pan if necessary.

4 Meanwhile heat the oil or fat in a frying pan and cook the onion, garlic and celery gently, stirring frequently, until the onion is soft and translucent.

5 Stir the fried vegetables into the beans and push the piece of salt pork or ham well down in the middle of them. Bring back to the boil and continue to simmer, topping up the water as necessary, for a further 45 minutes or so until the beans are very tender. Add salt, if necessary, 15–20 minutes before the end of the cooking time.

6 Measure the rice into a pan with a cup and add 1½ times its volume of cold water, plus 1 tsp salt. Bring to the boil, stirring occasionally, then cover the pan tightly and leave over a very low heat for 12 minutes. Without lifting the lid, turn off the heat and leave the rice undisturbed for a further 12 minutes.

7 Lift the piece of salt pork or ham out from among the beans and dice it, removing the fat and rind. Drain the beans and correct the seasoning with plenty of black pepper and more salt if necessary. Stir the diced meat through the beans.

8 Fork up the rice to make it fluffy, stir in the parsley, then mound it in a warm serving dish and pour the beans over the top.

COOK'S TIP

The soaking and first fast boiling are a safety measure to eliminate toxins present in red kidney beans, so do not skip these steps.

The beans are just as good made the day before and reheated when you cook the rice. Indeed, some Cajun cooks say that this makes them taste even better.

Spiced Aubergine Fried in Cornmeal

SERVES 3–4

INGREDIENTS
1 large aubergine (eggplant)
salt
1 egg
120ml/4fl oz/½ cup milk
2.5ml/½ tsp paprika
2.5ml/½ tsp cayenne pepper
2.5ml/½ tsp freshly ground black pepper
2.5ml/½ tsp garlic salt
115g/4oz/1 cup fine cornmeal
oil, for deep-frying

1 Cut the aubergine into 1cm/½in thick slices. Sprinkle lightly with salt and stack them in a colander. Leave to stand in the sink to drain for 30 minutes, then wipe the slices dry on kitchen paper.

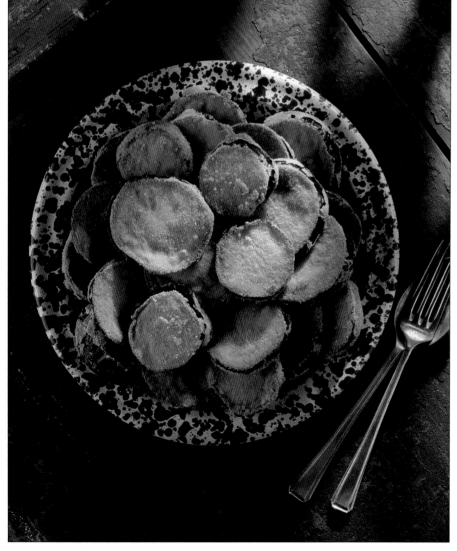

2 Beat the egg lightly in a shallow bowl with the milk, spices, pepper and garlic salt. Spread the cornmeal on a plate. Heat the oil for deep-frying.

3 Pass each slice of aubergine through the spiced egg mixture, allowing the excess mixture briefly to drip back into the bowl. Turn the slice in the cornmeal, then drop the slice immediately into the hot oil.

4 Fry 3 or 4 slices at a time, turning once, until they are golden on both sides. Drain thoroughly on kitchen paper and keep warm until all the slices are fried. Serve hot.

COOK'S TIP

The crisp aubergine slices are very good with grilled (broiled) meat, poultry or fish. They can also substitute for meat in a vegetarian meal.

Baked Sweet Potatoes

Sweet potatoes go well with the favourite Cajun seasonings: plenty of salt, white pepper as well as black and cayenne peppers, and lavish quantities of butter. Serve half a sweet potato per person as an accompaniment to meat, sausages or fish, or a whole one as a supper dish, perhaps topped with crisped and crumbled bacon and accompanied by a green side salad peppered with watercress or rocket (arugula).

SERVES 3–6

INGREDIENTS
3 pink-skinned sweet potatoes, each weighing about 450g/1lb
salt
75g/3oz/6 tbsp chilled butter, sliced
black, white and cayenne peppers

1 Wash the potatoes, leaving the skins wet. Rub salt into the skins, prick them all over with a fork, and place on the middle shelf of the oven. Turn on the oven at 200°C/400°F/Gas 6 and bake for about an hour, until the flesh yields and feels soft when pressed.

COOK'S TIP

Sweet potatoes cook more quickly than ordinary ones, and there is no need to preheat the oven.

2 The cooked potatoes can either be served in halves or whole. For halves, split each one lengthways and make close diagonal cuts in the flesh of each half. Then spread with slices of butter, and work the butter and seasonings roughly into the cuts with a knife point.

3 Alternatively, make an incision along the length of each potato if they are to be served whole. Open them slightly and put in butter slices along the length, seasoning with salt and the peppers.

Puddings

The Louisiana tooth is very sweet, and Louisianans do like to end a meal with a proper pudding. For our tastes, something as sweet, spicy and substantial as their bread pudding is a good finish to a light meal of soup or a salad – but if it still defeats delicate appetites, the leftovers will be just as satisfying the next day. Sticky pies and sumptuous cakes, usually featuring the favourite pecan nuts, are more special desserts, and ice creams are particularly popular on summer days when the humidity, as well as the temperature, soars.

Bread Pudding with Cranberry Sauce

This homely Louisiana classic may be made more elegant with creamy or rum-flavoured sauces. The scarlet tartness of cranberries makes an ideal foil to offset such a sweet and substantial pudding.

SERVES 6–8

INGREDIENTS
50g/2oz/4 tbsp butter, melted
750ml/1¼ pints/3 cups milk
3 eggs
*100g/3½oz/½ cup caster
   (superfine) sugar*
5ml/1 tsp vanilla extract
10ml/2 tsp ground cinnamon
2.5ml/½ nutmeg
*400g/14oz/9 cups cubed bread cut from a
   day-old French loaf (including crust)*
50g/2oz/½ cup chopped walnut kernels
75g/3oz/½ cup sultanas (golden raisins)

For the cranberry sauce
*350g/12oz/3 cups cranberries,
   fresh or frozen*
*finely grated peel and juice of
   1 large orange*
25g/1oz/2 tbsp caster (superfine) sugar

I Swirl the butter round a deep ovenproof pie dish or a roasting pan to coat it generously. Measure out the milk and pour any excess butter into it.

2 Beat the eggs with an electric whisk until light and frothy, then beat in the sugar, vanilla extract and cinnamon, and grate in the nutmeg. Finally, stir in the milk.

3 Pack the bread cubes into the prepared pie dish, sprinkling the walnuts and sultanas among them as you go.

4 Pour the custard mix over slowly and evenly, and leave to stand for 45 minutes, by which time only a little of the liquid should show around the rim.

5 Preheat the oven to 180°C/350°F/Gas 4. Bake the pudding in the oven for 45 minutes until risen and puffy, raising the heat to 200°C/400°F/Gas 6 for the last 10–15 minutes if the pudding is not turning golden on top.

6 To make the cranberry sauce, put the berries into a heavy pan with the orange peel and juice and the sugar.

7 Stir over a low heat until the sugar dissolves, then cook until the berries pop and the mixture thickens into a jam consistency. Serve hot or cold.

COOK'S TIP

Leftovers of both the pudding and the sauce are good cold or reheated.

Pecan Pie

This is a favourite pie all over the southern states, where pecans flourish. Louisiana is no exception.

SERVES 6

INGREDIENTS
For the pastry
200g/7oz/1¾ cups plain (all-purpose) flour
a pinch of salt
115g/4oz/½ cup butter
dry pulses or rice, for baking blind

For the filling
3 eggs
a good pinch of salt
5ml/1 tsp vanilla extract
200g/7oz/¾ well-packed cup soft dark
* brown sugar*
60ml/4 tbsp golden syrup or
* light corn syrup*
50g/2oz/4 tbsp butter, melted
115g/4oz/1 cup chopped pecan kernels,
* plus 12 pecan halves*

To serve
whipped cream or vanilla ice cream

1 Mix the flour with a pinch of salt, then rub in the butter with your fingertips to a coarse sand consistency. Add iced water a little at a time, mixing first with a fork, then with your hand, until the mixture gathers into a dough. Be sparing with the water.

2 Wrap the dough in cling film (plastic wrap) and refrigerate for 30–40 minutes. Preheat the oven to 190°C/375°F/Gas 5 for 20 minutes before you bake the tart.

3 Grease a 20–23cm/8–9in loose-based flan tin (pan). Roll out the pastry to line the tin, pressing it gently into place with your fingers.

4 Run the rolling pin over the top of the tin to sever the surplus pastry.

5 Prick the pastry base and line with foil. Fill it with dry pulses or rice and bake blind for 15 minutes, then remove the foil and pulses and bake for a further 5 minutes. Take the pastry case from the oven and lower the oven heat to 180°C/350°F/Gas 4.

6 Meanwhile, to make the filling, beat the eggs lightly with the salt and vanilla extract, then beat in the sugar, syrup and melted butter. Finally, mix in the chopped pecans.

7 Spread the mixture in the half-baked pastry case and bake for 15 minutes, then take it from the oven and stud with the pecan halves in a circle.

8 Return to the oven and bake for a further 20–25 minutes, until a thin metal skewer pushed gently into the centre comes out clean, with no uncooked mixture attached.

9 Cool the pie for 10–15 minutes and serve it warm with whipped cream or a scoop of vanilla ice cream.

COOK'S TIP

The corn syrup American cooks use in their pie filling is not widely available outside the US. Substitute golden syrup. You can, however, find corn syrup in the larger department store food halls in major cities.

Pralines

Pronounced with a long 'a' and the stress on the first syllable, these resemble puddles of nut fudge more than the crunchy toffee pools or hazelnut chocolates Europeans think of as pralines. In Louisiana they are eaten as a dessert or whenever it seems a good idea to have something sweet with a cup of coffee.

MAKES ABOUT 30 PIECES

INGREDIENTS
225g/8oz/2 cups pecan halves
450g/1lb/2 well-packed cups soft light brown sugar
200g/7oz/1 cup granulated (white) sugar
300ml/10fl oz/1¼ cups double (heavy) cream
175ml/6fl oz/¾ cup milk
5ml/1 tsp vanilla extract

1 Roughly chop half the pecans and set all the nuts aside. Grease and line 2–3 baking sheets with non-stick baking parchment.

2 Stir the brown and white sugars, cream and milk together in a heavy pan over a medium heat. Stir constantly until the mixture reaches 119°C/238°F or the soft-ball stage (*see* Cook's Tip).

3 Remove from the heat immediately and beat with an electric beater or a balloon whisk until the mixture loses its sheen and becomes creamy in texture and grainy-looking. This could take 15 minutes by hand or about 5 minutes with an electric beater.

4 Stir in the vanilla and both chopped and unchopped nuts, and drop tablespoons of the mixture on to the lined baking sheets, allowing it to spread of its own accord. Leave to cool and set at room temperature. Store between layers of greaseproof paper in a container with a tight-fitting lid.

COOK'S TIP

A mixture has reached the soft-ball stage when a teaspoonful dropped into cold water quickly sets to a soft ball. As this stage approaches, a spoonful of the mixture dribbled on the surface of the mixture in the pan will hold its trail. Test frequently towards the end of the cooking time unless you are using a sugar thermometer.

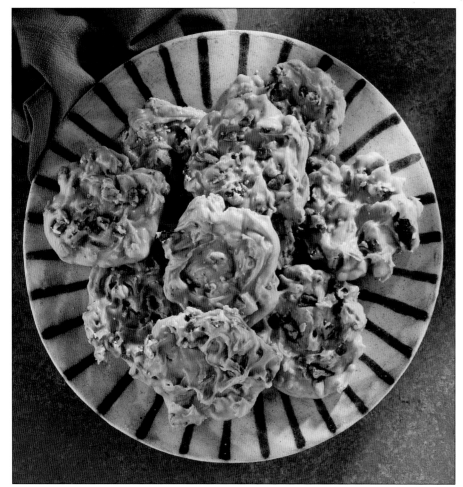

Bananas Foster

A now-famous dessert named after Dick Foster, who was on the Vice Committee and therefore in charge of cleaning up the French Quarter of New Orleans in the 1950s.

SERVES 4

INGREDIENTS
75g/3oz/⅓ cup soft light brown sugar
½ tsp ground cinnamon
½ tsp grated nutmeg
50g/2oz/4 tbsp butter
4 tbsp banana liqueur
5 tbsp dark rum
4 firm bananas, peeled and halved lengthways
4 scoops firmly frozen vanilla ice cream

1 Mix the sugar, cinnamon and nutmeg together. Melt the butter in a heavy frying pan and add the sugar and spice mixture.

2 Add the liqueur and rum, and stir over the heat until the sauce is syrupy.

COOK'S TIP

You can ring the changes with praline or walnut ice creams.

3 Add the bananas and heat through, turning to coat with the sauce.

4 Tilt the pan if you are cooking over gas to set light to the sauce. If your stove is electric, light the sauce with a match. Hold the pan at arm's length while you do this.

5 As soon as the flames die down, put 2 pieces of banana on each plate with a scoop of ice cream between them. Pour on the sauce and serve immediately.

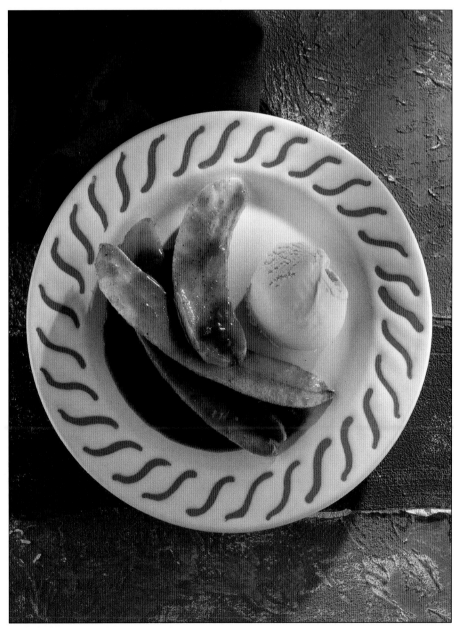

Coffee Ice Cream with Caramelized Pecans

SERVES 4–6

INGREDIENTS

For the ice cream
300ml/10fl oz/1¼ cups milk
15ml/1 tbsp demerara (raw) sugar
25g/1oz/6 tbsp finely ground coffee or
   1 tbsp instant coffee granules or powder
1 egg, plus 2 yolks
300ml/10fl oz/1¼ cups double
  (heavy) cream
15ml/1 tbsp caster (superfine) sugar

For the pecans
115g/4oz/1 cup pecan halves
50g/2oz/4 tbsp soft dark brown sugar

1 Heat the milk and demerara sugar to boiling point. Remove from the heat and sprinkle on the coffee. Leave to stand for 2 minutes, then stir, cover and cool.

2 In a heatproof bowl, beat the egg and extra yolks until thick and pale.

3 Strain the coffee mixture into a clean pan, heat to boiling point, then pour over the eggs in a steady stream, beating hard all the time.

4 Set the bowl over a pan of gently simmering water and stir until the mixture thickens. Cool, then chill in the refrigerator.

5 Whip the cream with the caster sugar. Fold it into the coffee custard and freeze in a covered container. Beat twice at hourly intervals, then leave to freeze firm.

6 To caramelize the nuts, preheat the oven to 180°C/350°F/Gas 4. Spread the nuts on a baking sheet in a single layer. Put them into the oven for 10–15 minutes to toast until they release their fragrance. Do not allow them to burn.

7 On top of the stove, dissolve the brown sugar in 2 tbsp water in a heavy pan, shaking the contents over a low heat until the sugar dissolves completely and the syrup clears.

8 When the syrup begins to bubble, add the toasted pecans and cook for a minute or two over a medium heat until the syrup coats and clings to the nuts.

9 Spread the nuts on a lightly oiled baking sheet, separating them with the tip of a knife, and leave to cool. Store when cold in an airtight container if they are not to be eaten on the same day.

10 Transfer the ice cream from the freezer to the refrigerator 30 minutes before scooping to serve, each portion topped with caramelized pecans.

COOK'S TIP

You can serve good-quality shop-bought ice cream with the same nutty garnish.

Watermelon Sherbet

A pretty pink sherbet that makes a light and refreshing dessert, this could appear before the main course to cleanse the palate at a grand dinner.

SERVES 6

INGREDIENTS
1kg/2¼lb piece watermelon
200g/7oz/1 cup caster (superfine) sugar
juice of 1 lemon
2 egg whites
mint leaves, to decorate

1 Cut the watermelon into wedges, then cut it away from the rind, cubing the flesh and picking out all the seeds.

2 Purée three-quarters of the flesh in a food processor or blender, but mash the last quarter on a plate – this will give the sherbet more texture.

3 Stir the sugar with the lemon juice and 120ml/4fl oz/½ cup cold water in a heavy pan over very low heat until the sugar dissolves and the syrup clears.

4 Mix all the watermelon and the syrup in a large bowl and transfer to a freezer-proof container.

5 Freeze for 1–1½ hours, until the edges begin to set. Beat the mixture, return to the freezer and freeze for a further 1 hour.

6 When the hour is up, whisk the egg whites to soft peaks. Beat the iced mixture again and fold in the egg whites. Return to the freezer for a further 1 hour, then beat once more and freeze firm.

7 Transfer the sherbet from the freezer to the refrigerator for 20–30 minutes before it is to be served. Serve in scoops, decorated with mint leaves.

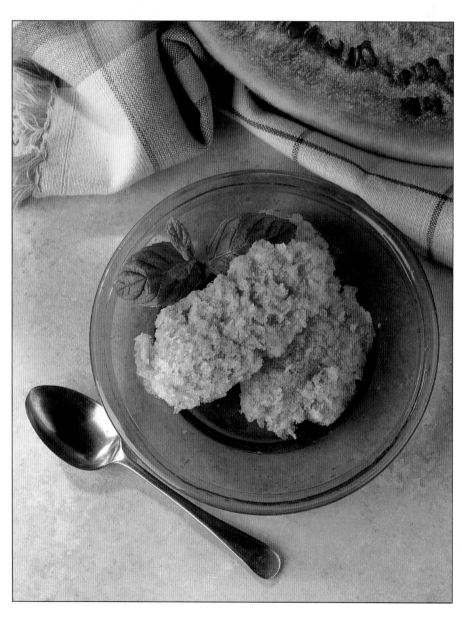

Creole Ambrosia

This refreshing cold, fruity pudding can be made at any time of year.

SERVES 6

INGREDIENTS
6 oranges
1 coconut
25g/1oz/2 tbsp caster (superfine) sugar

1 Peel the oranges removing all white pith, then slice thinly across the fruit, picking out seeds with the point of a knife. Do this on a plate to catch the juice.

2 Pierce the 'eyes' of the coconut and drain the liquid for use in another recipe. Crack open the coconut with a hammer. (This is best done outside on a stone surface.)

COOK'S TIP

Using mango instead of oranges makes the dessert more exotic but less authentic.

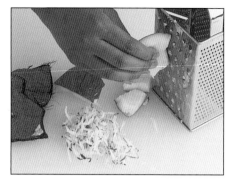

3 Peel the coconut with a sharp knife, then grate half the flesh coarsely, either on a hand grater or using the grating blade of a food processor.

4 Layer the coconut and orange slices in a glass bowl, starting and finishing with the coconut. After each orange layer, sprinkle on a little sugar and pour over some of the reserved orange juice.

5 Leave the dessert to stand for 2 hours before serving, either at room temperature or, in hot weather, keep it refrigerated.

Pecan Nut Divinity Cake

SERVES 6–8

INGREDIENTS
275g/10oz/2½ cups pecan nuts
350g/12oz/3 cups plain (all-purpose) flour
7.5ml/1½ tsp baking powder
2.5ml/½ tsp salt
225g/8oz/1 cup unsalted butter,
  at room temperature
400g/14oz/2 cups caster (superfine) sugar
5 eggs
225ml/8fl oz/1 cup milk
5ml/1 tsp vanilla extract

For the divinity icing
350g/12oz/3 cups icing (confectioners')
  sugar
3 egg whites, at room temperature
2 drops vanilla extract

1 Toast the pecans in batches in a heavy pan over a high heat, tossing regularly until they darken and give off a toasted aroma. Cool, then chop coarsely.

2 Preheat the oven to 180°C/350°F/ Gas 4. Oil and lightly flour three 23cm/9in diameter cake tins (pans). Sift the flour, baking powder and salt together. Toss half the pecans in 2 tbsp of the flour mixture. Reserve the remaining nuts for decoration.

3 Cream the butter and caster sugar together until pale and fluffy and add the eggs, one at a time, beating well after each addition.

4 Mix the milk with the vanilla extract. Stir the flour into the creamed mixture in 3 batches, alternating with the milk. Finally fold in the floured nuts.

5 Pour the cake mixture into the prepared cake tins and bake in the oven for 30 minutes, or until the tops are golden and the cakes have left the sides of the tins. Remove the cakes from the oven and leave to cool in the tins for 5 minutes before turning out on to a wire rack to cool completely.

6 To make the divinity icing, sift the icing sugar into a bowl, add the egg whites and set the bowl over a pan of boiling water. Whisk the mixture for 5–10 minutes until stiff peaks form.

7 Add the vanilla extract. Remove the bowl from the pan and continue whisking for a further 2–3 minutes. Working very quickly, sandwich the cake layers together with some of the icing, sprinkling each layer with some of the reserved pecans.

8 Ice the top and sides of the assembled cake and sprinkle the remaining nuts over the top to decorate.

Index